LIFE IN BLACK & WHITE

BY:

WILLIAM D. GORDON

DEDICATION

THIS IS FOR MY WIFE BARBARA WHO SPENT COUNTLESS LONELY DAYS AND NIGHTS WORRYING THAT I WOULD NOT MAKE IT HOME FROM THE "MEAN STREETS" OF BALTIMORE. SHE FINALLY GOT SO TIRED OF ME NOT TELLING HER WHAT WAS HAPPENING AT WORK THAT SHE GOT A JOB AS A 9-1-1 OPERATOR SO SHE COULD BETTER UNDERSTAND ME.

I WOULD ALSO LIKE TO ACKNOWLEDGE ALL OF THE MEN AND WOMEN THAT I WORKED WITH OVER THE YEARS. THE HEROES THAT GIVE THEIR LIVES IN THE LINE OF DUTY ARE ALWAYS HONORED (AND RIGHTLY SO) BUT SO OFTEN WE FAIL TO HONOR THOSE WHO SUFFER BOTH PHYSICALLY AND EMOTIONALLY FOR THE REST OF THEIR LIVES DUE TO THEIR DEDICATION TO THE CITIZENS THEY SERVED.

CONTENTS

INTRODUCTION

On the following pages you will read some of my exploits over the years. In typical cop fashion I have found humor where most "normal people" find consternation. I leave untold many of those stories which I have so efficiently buried to escape the pain; stories of watching fellow officers dying; my lifelong friend Ron Tracy being shot to death by a bystander while handling a minor traffic accident; just because he was a cop; children dead or dying in my arms. These are not the stories I want to tell, nor the ones my readers need to hear.

You will also notice a lack of profanity herein. This is intentional as I have never seen the need to use it myself and have no desire to repeat it from others. If this detracts from the "reality" I apologize in advance. You will hopefully notice I make prolific use of sarcasm. I have learned over the years (mostly from looks of disbelief) that not everyone understands sarcasm. As you read these adventures pay close attention to statements that seem ludicrous on the surface. There is a very good chance that I am employing sarcasm. For instance, in one account I question the integrity of the Mayor and follow that by stating that it was a good career move – that my friend is sarcasm.

As I was writing this I thought to myself (on several occasions) that I really shouldn't have done that. In some cases there was an abuse of power, and in others it was just plain stupid. There is a saying, "it is what it is". Looking back I could have done some things differently, but then again who among us wouldn't like a second chance?

Before we get into the actual incidents let me set the stage a bit. Baltimore City (for those of you who don't know it) is a port city. During the 1970's the three main industries that supported her were the port, the steel mills and the General Motors plant. With a population of over 800,000 residents that grew to over a million during the day there were on average 300 cops on patrol per shift (that's one cop for every 3,333 people). The social climate in 1975 was in turmoil. The "peace & love" generation of the 1960's turned suddenly violent in the 1970's. Riots, demonstrations and bombings became widespread. The climate within the police department was also chaotic. With the rookies almost outnumbering the veterans; women just starting to be hired as street cops (not "matrons" as in the past) and the number of black officers increasing, the status quo was out the window. If there is one thing a police department hates its change. This was change on a level never before witnessed. Prior to this it was common practice for the experienced officers to completely ignore the rookies. They had to first prove themselves to become an accepted member of the squad. I got my first look at racism from a few of the old timers when I arrived at the district. I say first look because I was either too innocent or blind growing up, but until that time the thought of something like this never entered my mind. Ron, my best friend at the academy was one of the nicest guys you would ever want to meet. He was a short black man with an infectious smile and an easy manner. When we graduated from the academy and were assigned to the Southeast District his nickname in the squad of old timers was "little spook". Thankfully, times have changed for the better.

IN THE BEGINNING....

My career with the Baltimore Police Department began on September 19, 1974. I did not present a very imposing figure  at 6'1" and only 140 lbs. Although endowed with reasonable intelligence and fairly good common sense I was very shy and lacked the "street smarts" of most city kids my age. I had grown up in northern Baltimore City in a neighborhood known as Hampden. I attribute my naiveté and lack of a juvenile arrest record to my shyness which kept me alone most of the time. I was fortunate enough to find some decent friends in my teen years that, unlike some of our peers, stayed out of trouble most of the time. The kids I hung out with as a teenager were a bit older than I, and I watched several of them join the Police Department as they turned twenty-one. I was a pretty typical teenager at the time, long hair, beard, jeans; the standard uniform of the culture that abhorred uniforms. I had no real direction in life, no real idea what I wanted or where I was going.

Isn't it strange how one seemingly small decision can change the course of one's life? Summer, 1974 was another typical hot and humid one in Baltimore City. The weather conditions only added to the tension already brewing between the rank and file in the PD and the city fathers. The outcome, no one would have predicted was a police strike.

On July 1, 1974 three thousand city sanitation workers, jail guards, and other non-police employees went on strike. The police did not join in at this time, but they did begin a work slow-down. Police officers wrote long and detailed reports on pennies found on the sidewalk and turned cigarette butts over to the police lab for drug analysis. Once they joined the strike however, it is estimated that nearly 1,300 of the 2,300 City police officers went on strike. Non-striking officers worked seven days a week in twelve hour shifts. Officers who did not strike were chastised for the decision by fellow officers. The city was not a safe place during this time; there was looting in the commercial district; fires ran 150% above normal. Within the first two days of the strike at least two hundred stores were looted. The city and state officials maintained a solid front against compromising and refused to make a settlement that gave strikers amnesty. The governor (Marvin Mandel) ordered one hundred fifteen state troopers into the city to help.

In an effort to stop the strike on July 13, Chief Judge Robert C. Murphy threatened to jail striking employees. The AFSCME was fined $10,000, and lost their collective bargaining agent status with the police department. The department fired over two hundred of the strike leaders outright; while hundreds more received severe disciplinary action.

During this time I was attending the Community College of Baltimore and had no plans or aspirations to join the police department.

I was a long haired, bearded motorcycle riding "hippy" student more interested in joining the Students for a Democratic Society than the police department.

Suddenly, the police department needed to hire hundreds of people in a real hurry. I was working part time at a gas station making $1.82 an hour pumping gas and changing oil in a grease pit. Surely being a cop and making $9,400 ($4.70 an hour) a year would be better than that. I figured I'd do it for the summer and then go back to school.

On September 9, 1974 I was sworn in as a Baltimore City Police Officer. I was ordered to report for the next academy class which started in October. The academy was in complete disarray. It went from graduating one or two classes a year to starting one new class a month. The sudden ramp up did not go smoothly. My class was 74-9, the 9th class started in 1974. The first day we were introduced to our class advisor – Sgt Scottie McDonald. Before the first week was gone the Sergeant had been replaced by Officer George Eckert. This was the first class to have a Police Officer as its advisor. Fortunately for us, George was a gem (and one of the funniest people I've ever met).

Having never been in the military I had no idea what to expect from a paramilitary organization. I had seen enough in the movies (this was before all of those "Police Academy" movies) to understand that I better have my uniform pressed, my shoes shined and my brass polished.

I was also determined to remain in the background and not attract any attention. This plan was suddenly dashed after the first weekly exam. I scored one hundred and was made a squad leader. You could fit what I knew about leadership on the head of a pin and still have room for the Declaration of Independence! I am happy to say, however that I did not lose a single member of my squad to enemy fire.

I found my twenty weeks in the academy interesting if not terribly relevant. Just as the public school systems of today are forced to teach to the test to receive federal funding, the police academy was forced to teach the subjects mandated by the Maryland Police Training Commission. In class after class the instructor would say, "Once you get out on the street you need to forget about all of this garbage." The self defense tactics classes were woefully inadequate. The various moves and tactics would be demonstrated a couple of times and then "practiced" a couple of times. That was it. It was expected that, months later in the heat of battle you would remember just how that hold was supposed to be applied. More often than not you resorted to your best home run swing with you nightstick!

The academic classes were taught through the Community College of Baltimore and received college credit. The downside was that we were being taught about real life situations by people who had never been in those situations themselves. These college professors were never asked to teach In-Service classes for experienced officers because they would be laughed out of the classroom.

So, every day for twenty weeks we sat and listened to the theory about subjects that we would have to practice once we graduated. Every week we were tested on our knowledge of these subjects and every week I came out at the top of the class. As we drew closer to graduating we were informed that the person with the highest score would be required to give a speech at the graduation. As I was extremely shy I knew there was no way I could stand up in front of hundreds of people (including the entire command staff) and give a speech. The only way out was to let someone else score higher. From that day on I purposely chose wrong answers on the tests. It was still very close; Chris Kunkle came out number one by four hundredths of a point. He gave a terrific speech too by the way.

As a final point to help you better understand my world I would like to briefly address the subject of integrity in the police department. I have been asked numerous times by civilians about how wide spread corruption was within the Baltimore Police Department. I am certain these questions were spawned by the Hollywood depiction of cops on "the take". I can state without hesitation that in my twenty five years at BPD (1974 to 1999) I never witnessed a culture of corruption (I cannot speak to the years since I left). Did I see corrupt officers, of course. However, these were the exception rather than the rule and they were, without exception dealt with in a judicious manner. The average citizen has no idea of the pressure and temptation that officers face on a daily basis. To add to this, the definition of corruption is a moving target. During my years there the simple act of accepting a free cup of coffee went from acceptable to a "bribe" and then back to acceptable again.

Officers who are poorly paid are routinely faced with confiscating large sums of money and valuables. Try to put yourself in their place - you have overdue bills and your kids need school clothes. Suddenly you find yourself holding thousands of dollars with no "rightful owner". What would you do? You'll see what I did in "What The Heck?" later in this book. My point is not to justify corruption, just put it in perspective. Officers are offered "gifts" from business owners all of the time. Are they bribes or expressions of gratitude? Suspects lie both in court and to Internal Affairs and always seem to get away with it. Day in and day out police officers see the worst society has to offer. Is it any wonder that some begin to blur and then cross the line? There are three areas that ensnare officer above all others. We have discussed money; the others are alcohol and sex. It was not uncommon for me to be propositioned at least once a night on the midnight shift. There are cop "groupies', women seeking protection or those that are just plain lonely. You may think I'm exaggerating but I assure you I am not. I also am not vain enough to think it had anything to do with me personally. Once I transferred to Vice I was the same guy (maybe even better looking with the long hair and beard) but not one proposition the entire time I was not in uniform. The thought I would like to leave you with is that cops are human. They have the same wants, needs and desires that the average citizen has. They are rightly held to a higher standard (even as the hiring standards are relaxed).

As you read this book, watch your local news or see your local police doing their duty try to keep this scripture from Luke 6:37 in mind: *"Moreover, stop judging, and you will by no means be judged; and stop condemning, and you will by no means be condemned. Keep on forgiving, and you will be forgiven"*.

FIELD TRAINING

In order to better understand the personality of the Officer W.D. Gordon who first hit the streets as a Trainee in December 1974 I offer the following:

Police trainees in those days spent several weeks in the academy and then went on the street with a Field Training Officer (FTO) while still wearing the khaki uniform that made us look more like UPS drivers than cops.

The first night in field training, I was working the Howard Street commercial area with Officer Chuck Walker, a short, thin, red-haired cop who seemed to know everyone. Not long before I was assigned as his latest trainee, Officer Walker had distinguished himself in, not one but two shootouts. In the first one he foiled the armed robbery of an eating establishment while off duty. There he was, in civilian clothes just trying to eat a late supper in peace after a long day at work.

As he slowly, methodically shoveled mashed potatoes and something vaguely resembling roast beef into his mouth, he looked up to see two men. One was standing by the door as a lookout while the other held a gun on the cashier demanding money. Carefully, so as not to draw attention to himself, Officer Walker removed his off-duty weapon (a puny thirty-eight caliber five shot Smith & Wesson revolver) from his ankle holster.

The suspect at the register catches this movement out of the corner of his eye and turns toward him while cocking his revolver. With no time to take cover Officer Walker fires his first shot from under the table. In one fluid motion he throws the table aside, jumps up and rushes the suspect with the gun as he continues firing. The suspect is struck in the gun hand and left side and, as he goes down his gun slides across the tile floor toward the other suspect. Officer Walker is able to reach the gun before it falls into the hands of the other suspect, but he is not out of danger yet. The second suspect rushes Officer Walker in an attempt to wrestle the gun from him and, no doubt use it on him. Officer Walker sidesteps and strikes the suspect hard in the chest with the butt of the revolver. This blow knocks the wind from the suspect and causes him to fall next to his accomplice. Now that both suspects are down, Officer Walker identifies himself as a Police Officer.

Did you happen to notice here that there was no, "Police Officer, drop your weapon" shouted prior to action being taken? I told you this was a true story – not a Hollywood production. Anyway, while this whole Wild West shootout is going down another employee is on the phone to 9-1-1. Nobody knows that an off-duty officer is involved, but the 9-1-1 operator hears the shootout while she is taking the call. Now, with two suspects on the floor to control Officer Walker has to worry about being shot by the responding officers as they converge on the scene of an armed robbery – shots fired! It was very likely his red hair that saved him.

Although this was not his shift, the responding officers had seen this short redheaded officer at shift changes just often enough to cause them to hesitate before shooting a man that, to all intents and purposes appears to be an armed robber. Once bona fides are established the suspects are sent off to the hospital to treat their wounds. On examining the suspect's gun Officer Walker finds that the trigger had been pulled twice, striking and denting the primers on both rounds. Neither of them fired! Chuck escaped unscathed that night; but not so on another night.

Officer Walker was on his foot post when the call came out for a man with a gun at Baltimore and Gay Streets. Responding quickly he located a witness who described two men and directed him to one of the night clubs in the 400 block of East Baltimore Street. Entering the dark night club from the brightly lit street placed him at a disadvantage. The two men seated at the bar had already adjusted to the low light levels. Seeking to even the odds a bit Officer Walker and his backup officer ordered the suspects to a room in the back where the lighting was better. As they walked down the hall toward the room one of the suspects spun around and opened fire on the officers. Officer Walker was struck in the right arm and his partner was struck in both legs. Though both seriously wounded the officers were able to return fire killing one suspect and seriously wounding the other. From that day on, for as long as I knew Chuck the sweater he was wearing that night became a part of his uniform. He called it his lucky sweater. I guess luck is all in how you look at it.

Although Chuck Walker was my official Field Training Officer (FTO) another member of the squad became my unofficial FTO. Officer John Heiderman was also very influential in my early – formative stage. An interesting side note here – both Officer Walker and Officer Heiderman were shot in the line of duty. Thankfully, both recovered from their wounds. They were able to pass on their combined wisdom and experience to me so that I did not follow in their footsteps. For that I am eternally grateful.

My first night with Officer Walker would not include any shootouts; however it was to be an exciting night for me. While walking the downtown business district we came upon a fight on the street which had just ended and Chuck told me to break up the crowd. I sort of apprehensively walked into the middle of them and politely asked them to leave. After a couple of minutes Chuck could no longer contain himself (I was having no effect at all) he walked over and shouted, "Hey! People, the Padre there in the brown uniform is available to take your confessions. If you don't want to confess get the heck off my street!" For the rest of my field training I was called the Padre.

DON'T MESS WITH LITTLE OLD LADIES

Upon graduating the Police Academy I was assigned to a Federal Foot Post in the Southeast District. A Federal Foot Post was a "new" concept in 1975. It was, in effect the taxpayers of the entire country funding an officer on foot patrol in a Baltimore neighborhood through grants to the city. You see, police crime fighting strategy is cyclical. Police had historically walked a "beat" in urban areas. It was not until the 1950's and 1960's that police officers drove around in cars. Prior to that, police cars were used by command, supervision and special units like traffic patrols. As the country prospered after WWII and there was money to be spent the "great thinkers" in law enforcement decided that officers in patrol cars could respond faster and be "omnipresent" so criminals would never know when they would show up, thereby reducing crime. The other benefit to this was that they would need fewer police to cover the same geographic area. It took a couple of decades (until the next set of "great thinkers" was in power) to realize that this concept turned the officer from a friendly neighborhood fixture that was always there when you needed him to a mysterious person who swooped in, defused the situation, sent criminals off to jail and then vanished. The new set of "great thinkers" decided that it would be conducive to the general feeling of safety and well being of the community to have officers on foot in certain neighborhoods. So, as a result of this "new" concept I began my career walking the cold streets of Baltimore City in February 1975.

On my first day I was given no instruction what-so-ever (everyone in this squad was an old timer except Ron Burke and me). I was dropped off and told to be on the same corner at three-thirty pm to be picked up, if I wasn't there I could walk back. My beat encompassed an eight square block area and contained one bank, two bars, a drug store, a fruit stand, several other businesses and a couple of hundred row homes. The residents were hard working blue collar workers for the most part. Many worked on the waterfront or the steel mills. The area to the north was changing and not for the better. The Urban Flight phenomenon had turned many of those houses into rentals. The lack of pride in ownership was becoming obvious; to the point that some were vacant and more than a few had become havens for drug dealers. It was my job to keep that from moving further south into the currently stable neighborhood. That's right, one cop walking eight hours a day was supposed to turn the tide of urban blight.

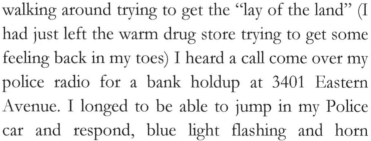

Anyway, back to my first day on the job. As I was walking around trying to get the "lay of the land" (I had just left the warm drug store trying to get some feeling back in my toes) I heard a call come over my police radio for a bank holdup at 3401 Eastern Avenue. I longed to be able to jump in my Police car and respond, blue light flashing and horn blaring; City Police cars had no sirens in 1975 (another act of political genius).

Alas, I had no Police car to jump into and running down the street with my flashlight on making siren (horn) noises was out of the question, so I listened as the call developed. I was walking west on Fayette Street when I heard the first unit call 10-23 (on-scene) and announce that there had indeed been a holdup. While I waited for a description (more out of curiosity than necessity as I was stuck way up there on foot) I heard the squealing of tires and the sound of a car striking something. I looked up Fayette Street to see that a car had failed to negotiate a turn onto Port Street and struck the corner house. I ran toward the accident to determine if medical attention was required. When the driver saw me coming he jumped out of the passenger side of the car and started running south on Port Street. My first thought was that he was pretty stupid to run from me because I was there to help him. He had only taken a

 few steps when a loud bang came from a bag he was carrying. Red smoke and dye flew in every direction. All of a sudden it was raining red money! I wasn't quite sure what to make of this; it was certainly very odd (no one had mentioned dye packs and their significance while I was in the Academy). I wasn't sure if I should chase the man or guard the money. Why had his money blown up anyway? At the same time a description of the hold-up man was coming over the radio along with the fact that he had been given a "dye pack". WOW! This was the guy and that was the dye pack! Forget the money; I wanted to catch a bank robber on my first day on the job. I got on the radio and informed the dispatcher that I was in foot pursuit of the bank robbery suspect (everyone is a suspect until proven guilty in a court of law).

I chased him south on Port Street from Fayette and was gaining on him when he turned and pointed his gun at me. Try to remember, I was a rookie and had not watched a lot of cop shows, so I was not prepared to shoot the gun from his hand the instant he turned. It is often overlooked, especially by the "Monday morning quarterbacks" that a massive amount of data must be processed  in a split second in order to make a life or death decision at a time like this. My first concern was for the citizens in the area. An officer is responsible for each and every bullet he fires. Again, unlike the movies where they spray the area and hope to hit the suspect, in real live there are children playing and people on the streets going about their daily business. Also vital to the decision making process are the Federal, State and local laws as well as departmental policies applicable for that situation, add to that civil liability and you have a lot to process in a short period of time. I did a quick evaluation of the situation and, though I had my gun out, I couldn't fire at him because the street was full of kids playing. I took cover behind a parked car and he turned and began to run again. He cut down an alley, ran into a yard and then into the back door of a house.

In general, the back yards of Baltimore row houses are nothing to brag about. They are usually just concrete slabs with a potpourri of stuff that won't fit into the house. On occasion they are even trash strewn and rat infested. Not this one, it was obvious that someone spent a lot of time and care beautifying this small patch of real estate.

There were planters and yard ornaments tastefully arranged and separated by a picket fence lined walkway. The house too showed a pride of ownership. I cautiously approached the door as I didn't know if he had continued to run or was waiting inside to ambush me. I heard a woman scream and the suspect yell for her to shut up or he would shoot her. This wasn't working out the way I wanted. With the suspect inside holding hostages I would have to call for the Quick Response Team (QRT or SWAT) and they would get to have all of the fun. I heard a lot of commotion inside the house; the suspect was yelling and now two women were screaming. The tone had changed however and it sounded like the suspect was on the defensive. Just then the door burst open and the suspect came running out followed by the two elderly women, one holding a butcher knife and the other an iron skillet. I grabbed the suspect, threw him to the ground and handcuffed him. The old ladies were hitting and kicking at him the whole time. My backup arrived while this was going on and held the ladies back while I got the suspect into the "patty wagon". One of the old ladies walked over to me and handed me the suspect's gun saying, "That no good SOB had a lot of nerve breaking into my house and scaring us like that. Looky here, he didn't even have the sense to use a real gun neither." Sure enough what she had handed me was a realistic looking plastic toy gun. For the next month or so I got calls to all of the local stores for kids trying to buy stuff with red money. What a start that was. I expected every day to be that much fun. Of course this is real life and not the movies so I spent a lot of quiet, boring days which I hated then and look back upon fondly now.

My second bank robbery happened just a few weeks later. This one was not quite as exciting but noteworthy nonetheless.

I was just starting my shift and was walking the neighborhood on Milton Avenue. It was a bright sunny morning and the temperatures had risen as we approached the middle of March. I had made a habit of carrying lollipops in my pocket to bribe the kids into telling me what was happening in the neighborhood (who broke a window, who stole a bike, etc). I also used them to reward the good kids. As I approached the corner of Milton and Orleans Streets one of the youngsters ran over to me and handed me a drawing he had done of me giving him a lollipop. It was a very cute drawing and I was touched by it (it hung on my refrigerator for months afterward). I was just enjoying the moment when a call came out for a holdup alarm at the Bradford Federal Savings & Loan at Fayette Street and Luzerne Avenue. I was a block and a half away on Orleans Street. When I arrived at the S&L I found the door locked and could see the manager and tellers in a group in the lobby. When the manager saw me he opened the door and informed me that they had in fact been robbed.

I went through all of the proper procedures (putting out a description, securing the crime scene and calling for the detectives). As this institution was not federally insured (S&L's were not covered under FDIC back then) there was no FBI investigation. The Criminal Investigation Division - Robbery detectives arrived in about twenty minutes and took over the investigation. There had been no dye pack given but the teller was sure she had seen the suspect before. The detectives transported her down to Headquarters (HQ) where she spent hours looking at "mug books" to no avail. The surveillance video was retrieved and found to be of little value.

Besides the tape (pre-digital) being very grainy the suspect was wearing a baseball cap and did not look up so the camera could catch his face. It seemed as if this one would go unsolved. That is until two days later.

Once again I was diligently patrolling my post when the holdup alarm came in for Bradford Federal Savings & Loan. I arrived within three minutes and found the manager waiting for me at the door. He related that the suspect had returned and gone to the same teller. This time however, instead of a holdup note he handed her his mortgage payment book and a stack of twenty dollar bills still in the S&L wrapper!

I obtained the name and address for the suspect (he lived just around the corner) and notified the Robbery detectives. They met me at the S&L and from there we went to the suspect's house. I was ordered to watch the back door as they went to the front. As they had not obtained a warrant there was no knocking down the front door and rushing in. The detectives knocked on the front door and announced themselves. Within a few seconds the suspect came rushing out the back door. I ordered him to the ground at gunpoint and he gave up without a fight. Two of the detectives came around and handcuffed him and then called for the other team to bring the car into the alley to transport the suspect to HQ.

A passing newspaper reporter grabbed his camera and took a shot of the suspect being loaded into the car. There I was, six weeks on the street and I was on the front page of the paper (looking like an innocent bystander). This should have opened my eyes to methods used by Detectives, but I was still far too trusting. I came to distrust Detectives later in my career as you will see.

LESSONS LEARNED

I only remained on the Federal Foot Post for six months. As soon as there was an opening in a patrol sector I jumped at it. I now happily patrolled a ten block by four block area in an honest to goodness police car. I was not in the squad very long when I learned first-hand that the so called "code of silence" was another one of those movie myths. It all started on a boring and quiet Sunday afternoon. I was working the Highlandtown business district. As I said the area was ten blocks by four blocks with the businesses being the focal point of the post (a post is the designation for a specifically defined area of responsibility). The rest of the post consisted of row houses occupied by mostly quiet, law abiding citizens. As most of the businesses were closed on Sunday there weren't many people on the street. You can only drive around in circles for so long until you start getting dizzy. For those of you who are not residents of Baltimore City and whose knowledge of police work has been gleaned from TV and movies an important piece of information to remember when reading these adventures is that Baltimore Police work alone. Each post is assigned a single officer alone in a single patrol car. This of course added to the aforementioned boredom.

The Star Wars movie had just been released and was showing at the Patterson Theater. There was a great deal of

hype and excitement about this new movie. It was all the rage and a special effects marvel for the time. It had never occurred to me to go to a movie while I was on-duty. The acting sergeant (OIC) Bill Roberts called for me to pick him up at the station due to a shortage of cars. He kept complaining about how bored he was and finally said we should go and watch the movie.

The Patterson was one of those elegant old movie houses built in the early 1900's. However, by 1975 it had obviously seen

better days. Unlike the mega theaters today there was only one screen, and it was huge. The theater had a high ceiling and had seating for about three hundred sixty customers.

The movie had just started when we quietly slipped in the back and took the two seats near the door. A couple of minutes into the movie a minor call came over the radio for another unit. Even though I had it turned down low it still sounded loud in the theater. Bill told me to turn it off. What? Turn off my radio while I'm on-duty? Yes, he insisted. Well, I was just a rookie and he was the acting sergeant so I turned my radio off as directed.

We enjoyed the movie and just as it was ending we slipped out ahead of the crowd. As we exited the theater I was shocked to see our lieutenant sitting on the hood of my car.

"We have been looking for you for over an hour!" the Lieutenant said icily. My mind was racing for an answer. Surely my OIC would speak up and tell the LT that going to the movie was his idea. At last Bill spoke up, "I know LT I've been looking everywhere for him too. I just found him in there watching the movie." I was stunned. I just stood there with my mouth open and nothing coming out. "Meet me in my office" the LT said as he got in his car and left. I turned to Bill and asked, "What was that!?" "Hey, there was no sense in both of us getting into trouble was there?" he replied.

All the way into the station I was contemplating my fate. Was the LT going to write me up and charge me? Would I be fired? After all, I was still on probation. It was the longest ride of my life.

By the time I walked into the station everyone knew what was happening. The Desk Sergeant just shook his head as I walked by. I never realized how long the hall to the Shift Commander's office was until I walked it that day. Everyone I encountered either chuckled or had a pained look on their face.

As I entered the office the LT looked up from his desk with that goofy grin he always wore (like in the picture) and held  something out to me. I took it and saw that it was an ear phone for the radio. "If you find that you must make a business check where your radio might disturb the other patrons wear this so you can still monitor the radio. That's all, get back out there and call back in service." Talk about dodging a bullet? I learned several very valuable lessons that day, not the least of which was how to be a good boss.

GRAVEYARD SHIFT

As I mentioned in the previous adventure, I had remained in the Foot Squad for six very long months until there was an opening in sector three that patrolled the Highlandtown area. On my first midnight shift in my new squad I drove around trying to learn the area while it was quiet so I would be

 prepared when the action started. At around three a.m. I was driving north in the Unit block North Conkling Street alongside the graveyard. Let me start off by explaining that I do not believe in ghosts. Having said that, a

graveyard at night with clouds passing over a full moon and a breeze rustling the trees is unsettling. As I gazed upon this eerie scene, suddenly I heard a woman's scream coming from inside the graveyard! I stopped the car and listened, surely I was mistaken. It was deathly quiet (pun intended) but after a moment I heard it again. It was definitely coming from inside the graveyard. I got on the radio and informed the dispatcher that I had heard screaming from the graveyard at Conklin and Baltimore Streets and I was going to investigate.

The graveyard was surrounded by a stone wall topped with a wrought iron fence; the gate of course was locked. I drove my car up onto the sidewalk next to the fence and by standing on the roof I was able to get over it.

I could still hear the screams somewhere out in the graveyard but there were no lights within; only the moon shining it's eerie light through the passing clouds sending the grave stones alternately into shadow and pale light.

Using my small flashlight I began the spine tingling task of searching for the damsel in distress among the headstones. The clouds were moving at a pretty good clip, so shadows were dancing across the headstones and monuments. I kept catching the movement out of the corner of my eye and half expecting someone to jump out at me (a live rapist not a spirit). In the distance behind me I saw one, and then two, and then all four of the other Sector Three units pull up on Conkling Street,  get out of their cars and stand there watching me. I thought this was odd for two reasons. First, I had quickly learned that after 3:00am the rest of the squad was "in the hole" (cop talk for a secluded place where you could meditate undisturbed) resting and they were not about to come out unless something serious was happening. I felt that a woman screaming in the graveyard was serious, but it didn't require the whole squad. The second thing I found odd was that they did not move to assist me; they just stood there smiling, talking and pointing.

Still trying to figure this out I continued my search. The graveyard was only about a block wide but had a bit of a rise before it ended. Suddenly, there in front of me was the answer to the strange behavior of my squad. I had reached the other side of the graveyard and there I saw about a dozen squealing pigs in their pens waiting to be "processed" at the Esskay meat processing plant. My damsel in distress turned out to be Ms. Piggy! Needless to say I was the butt of pig jokes for some time afterward. It's hard enough to be a rookie, but a rookie with my propensity to find unusual situations made it even worse.

That was not the last of my farm animal adventures. Although the following incidents took place at various times in my career I have included them out of sequence to get them out of the way all at once.

Handling farm animals is a call that city officers seldom receive. The closest your average city cop gets to a cow is the burger he gets at McDonald's. So, when a tractor trailer carrying a load of cows was involved in a traffic accident that set several cows to running loose on a city street it was sheer pandemonium. You would have thought that these poor, frightened cows constituted the running of the bulls. Officers who would face an angry mob of looters were running and hiding behind cars. Some tried to herd them with their cars which proved fruitless. Each time an officer would work up the courage to approach one of these monsters it would bawl loudly and take off at a run. Unfortunately, it always seemed to run toward a fellow officer. At one point an officer decided that these animals were posing a serious threat to the other officers and the general public.

It was inopportune that he did not make this decision until the local news crews were on the scene and set up. The officer drew his service weapon and, being careful of crossfire he shot the closest cow. Instead of the cow falling over and expiring as he expected the cow began running wildly toward other officers. These officers then drew their weapons and began firing also. In all, the cow was hit forty-six times out of sixty-eight shots fired. How the news crew, bystanders and the other officers escaped the fusillade is a miracle unto itself. How you can miss a target the size of a cow at close range is more of a mystery. Anyhow, the six o'clock news had a field day with that one. The entire district was the butt of many jokes for a long time afterward. A few years later we had a similar problem but with a happier ending.

Baltimore city still had horse drawn wagons selling produce and collecting junk even into the 1980's. These were

small wagons pulled by a single small horse. As a kid I can remember them coming through the neighborhood yelling, "Strawwberries! Cherrrries!" Or coming down the alley looking for scrap metal or other junk they could sell. I have no idea why; but they were known as Arabers (pronounced ay-rabbers).

It never fails, even think about how quiet a night you're having and how maybe you will get through the shift without something blowing up in your face and, guess what? Before you know it you're up to your neck in it. That is exactly how this night went.

It was about four a.m. as I was driving down the 1700 block of West Baltimore Street just trying to stay awake. It was a dark, moonless night and the breeze was blowing the trash around the street among the little dust devils. As I watched some newspaper captured by one of the little devils I saw something in the middle of the street up ahead. My eyes saw it but my brain refused to believe it. I probably did one of those classic movie moves; rubbing my eyes in case I was hallucinating. There, walking down the center line of Baltimore Street was a small horse. On the sidewalk I saw two more. They appeared to be window-shopping in the stores. I was reluctant  to put this one over the radio. I already had a reputation as a practical joker (why I don't know). Who exactly do you call for horses loose on a city street? Even if the Animal Shelter had someone working at this time of the morning how would they fit three horses into their little truck? As usual, the job fell on us.

I had no choice, there was no way I could round up these critters alone no matter how many westerns I had watched as a kid. I got on the radio and requested that two of my units meet me at my location. I may have to call for help but I didn't have to let the world know why. When they arrived and discovered the situation they too were dumbfounded. Even if we were able to corral these beasts what were we to do with them? After careful consideration we determined that we would need some rope and barricades. That meant calling for the Emergency Vehicle Unit (EVU). This is a specially equipped truck that carries just about anything an officer might need in an emergency. As soon as I asked for EVU the cops came out of the woodwork. Both adjoining districts responded to see what was going on. Once the EVU arrived we set up a makeshift corral with some barricades and set about lassoing the horses. This was nothing like the rodeos I'd seen in the movies. These little guys just stood there while we roped them and came along willingly as we led them to the corral. Fortunately, there was a Western District officer there who knew his post and had a good idea where they had escaped from. He was able to find the stable owner who responded and took the horses home. It just goes to show you; you have to be ready for anything when you are a city cop!

FATHER TIME

When you are a rookie everyone seems like an "old timer". The "old timer" in my first squad in patrol had been on for about twenty years when I got there. He was still there when I retired! His name was John. He was the cigar smoking, whiskey drinking, pot-bellied caricature of an old time cop. The thing that was hard for me to believe, and took a while to catch on to, was that John was the biggest and most successful womanizer in the district. With his craggy, weathered looks and easy laugh he could always brighten up the room.

My suspicions about John began on the third or fourth domestic call we went on together. He always sent me outside with the man (to get his story) while he stayed inside with the woman. If an arrest was dictated, I was always the one to take the guy in while John stayed at the house to console the woman. I asked another guy in the squad about this and he just laughed at me. He told me that I should just ask John why he worked this way. I didn't really think he would tell me but I decided to ask anyway. One quiet night on the midnight shift I caught John before he went in the "hole" and casually brought the subject up. He laughed his funny little laugh and did not respond. I persisted. "How am I to learn and become a good cop if you guys won't tell me anything" I complained. After thinking about it for a while he relented and related this story. Early in his career John was patrolling the waterfront when he observed a car parked with the windows steamed up. He approached the car, flung open the door and shined his flash light inside.

There he saw a young couple in the throes of passion. The sudden authoritative audience immediately ruined the young man's enthusiasm. John ordered the young man to get dressed and start walking or he would arrest him. After the guy was gone John got in and finished the job for him.

This was the beginning of his womanizing ways. From that he discovered his now tried and true method of handling domestics in the home. One night about eighteen years later John was checking all of the usual parking hideouts for young lovers and, as usual he found what he was looking for. He sent the young man on his way and got into the car with the young lady. She smiled brightly and said, "Hi Mr. John, remember me? You use to come by the house and visit my mom when I was a kid. She told me about the time that you caught her down here with her boyfriend. That was the year before I was born." John was stunned. As he looked more closely at the girl he thought he could see some of himself in her features. He told the girl to say hello to her mother and left in a hurry. He contemplated almost having sex with a girl that, in all likelihood was his own daughter. He made a promise to himself to be much more careful in the future. Over the years John became known as the father of Highlandtown; literally. However, he always made sure he knew the parentage of his conquests. I never heard of John pursuing a minor or an unwilling female. He just had such a way with women that they wanted to make him happy. I learned a lot from John over the years we worked together. Some I used to make me a better cop, others I used to make me a better investigator in Internal Affairs.

WHAT THE HECK?

It is very hard to make people understand just how bad the high rise projects in Baltimore were. Unless you actually went to one and experienced the sights (dirt, filth and hopelessness)  sounds (fussing & fighting, crying and gunshots) and smells (urine in elevators and trash in the halls) you just cannot imagine it. These high rise "prisons" were built in the 1960's in response to President Johnson's "Great Society" project. Envisioned as a kindness to those living in poverty it turned their lives into complete chaos. That, combined with the incentives given to single mothers (they got their own apartment and increased benefits) led to the decline of the family unit that is responsible for so many of the ills facing society today. That's all for the social commentary.

We had three of these twelve story apartment buildings in my sector in Southeast District. Unless a call to one of these hellholes was dispatched officers stayed as far from them as possible. Not me of course. On midnight shift when everything quieted down after the bars closed at two a.m. I would walk around and see what I could find. Without fail, I would walk up on unsuspecting residents who would look as if they had seen a ghost. All would be wide eyed and some would be rendered speechless. On one particularly pleasant summer night, I came out of the hall into the stairwell right in the middle of a crap (dice) game. The reaction was sheer disbelief. People froze where they were and just stared. It was an effort on my part not to laugh aloud at their reaction. Finally, in a stern voice I said, "Gentlemen, I do believe gambling is illegal in the city of Baltimore". That broke the spell. It was "buttholes and elbows" flying in all directions. I was left in a deserted stairwell with a set of dice and a

pile of money. It must have been the beginning of the month (when welfare checks come out) because the pot was pretty good sized. I scooped it up and took it down to Evidence Control as required by the rules and regulations of the department. I could tell as soon as I walked into the Evidence Control unit that I was not a welcome sight. When they found out I had money to turn in it got even chillier in there. You see the procedure for handling money required that each bill be laid out and photographed with the serial number clearly visible. As my submission consisted of mostly one-dollar bills, it took a while to accomplish this. While finalizing the paperwork they asked me for the name of the arrestee. I told them I did not arrest anyone so they asked who the money belonged to. When I informed them of the circumstances surrounding the money seizure their reaction was akin to the guys I found gambling.

They stood there, mouths open and speechless. Finally, one of them asked why I would bring the money to Evidence Control and turn it in under these circumstances. My answer, "Because the General Orders say so". *Life in Black & White*.

NIGHT COURT

Unlike the "Big Apple" (New York City), Baltimore City does not have night court. Before all of the District courts were consolidated, anyone arrested over night for a minor offense was held over for trial the next morning at the district's court room. This was what any resident of the city would expect for being arrested for drunk & disorderly conduct. John Wilkens however was not a resident of our fair city. He was in fact the quintessential New York loudmouth. Now John made a couple of mistakes one fateful night in October 1976. The first of which was to come to Baltimore. Once here he proceeded to get intoxicated in a local gin mill and as is so common of intoxicated people he proceeded to make a fool of himself.

I received the call at around one thirty a.m. for an intoxicated man in a bar on Fleet Street (Intoxicated man in a bar, how unusual). It had been a fairly busy start to the midnight to eight shift and I was not in the mood for foolishness. I was on-scene within a couple of minutes; traffic is pretty light at that time of the morning. I entered the front door of the bar expecting a "routine" bar fight but instead found Mr. Wilkens with his back to the wall and everyone in the bar trying to get to him. He was medium height with a stocky but muscular build. He was wearing a NY Yankees shirt and cutoff shorts. Apparently he had been in town for the Orioles/Yankee game earlier in the evening. The fact that the Orioles won contributed to his foul mood I'm sure.

First impressions not always being accurate, I thought he was the victim. I was soon to realize the error of this assumption.

In what was by now a practiced and polished routine I cleared the bar to remove the danger to Mr. Wilkens. It did not take long for me to regret that move. He began to lecture me in that obnoxious way so typical of New Yorker drunks. I had the great pleasure of listening to him berate my city, state, department, and yes even sweet wonderful me. After several attempts to persuade him to leave the bar and go home (preferably to New York) he informed me that if I did not leave he was going to inflict immediate and permanent physical injury upon my person. Taking exception to this I placed him under arrest. He howled and screamed as I handcuffed him and led him outside to the paddy wagon.

Some of the patrons had gathered outside to see what would happen and they cheered and applauded as I placed Mr. Wilkens in the wagon and slammed the door. They waved and shouted some choice words to him as he was taken away to the district lockup.

Mr. Wilkens continued his verbal abuse at the district. Deciding that enough was more than enough, I decided it was time to teach him a lesson, Baltimore style. In New York they don't have the finesse; the flair we possess here.

They would simply beat the tar out of him and be done with it. I achieved the same results without resorting to physical violence of any kind. Before the state consolidated the District Courts into a central location, each police station had their own court room. The one in the Southeast District was well appointed. It  contained about fifteen rows with wooden high backed benches for those who wished to view the proceedings as well as those awaiting trial that were out on bail and their family members and witnesses. The State's Attorney and state's witnesses (police mostly) sat at a table to the judge's right and the defense (accused and their lawyer if they had one) sat to the left. A long polished brass bar stood in front of these tables separating the prisoners from the judge. The prisoners in the cell block were led through a long hallway directly into the court room. With its high ceiling and floor to ceiling windows it was an impressive setup.

Officer John (our resident old timer) went into the judge's chambers and put on the judicial robes while I got everyone in the station house into the court room. With about ten officers (some in plain clothes) in the court room we had the Turn-key bring the prisoner in for "Night Court". I was sworn in and gave my testimony in great and flourishing detail. The "Judge", looking very stern, occasionally threw in a "tsk - tsk" for effect. Then, as if on cue a thunderstorm rolled in. The wind picked up followed by flashes of lightening and claps of thunder.

As the rain started to beat against the windows it was time for Mr. Wilkens to testify. His arrogance reigned supreme.

The "Judge" let him ramble on for a while and then in a performance worthy of an Oscar award he pronounced judgment. "Mr. Wilkens, please rise. I find it reprehensible that you would travel to our fair city and cause such pandemonium. We are not accustomed to this sort of behavior here. If we do not have swift, sure judgment in this case the entire city may fall into chaos.

It is with this in mind that I hereby remand you to the custody of the State Executioner who will carry out the sentence of death by electrocution immediately. May GOD have mercy on your miserable New York soul!"

As you might imagine, it was difficult for us to keep a straight face through this. Mr. Wilkens was miraculously transformed. He was suddenly sober and very civilized.

There was silence in the courtroom for about a minute until we could hold back no longer. Almost as one we broke down laughing. Mr. Wilkens was bewildered at first, but when Officer John removed the robe to reveal his uniform he knew he had been the victim of a world class hoax.

He began to laugh along with us (from relief more than anything else) until the whole room was rolling with laughter.

In the morning when it was time to go before the judge we had to assure Mr. Wilkens that this was the real thing. This time sentencing was a bit more lenient. He was given a $50 fine and court costs. Upon being sentenced he looked at the judge and said, "Is it for real this time?" Several stifled laughs were heard in the court room. The judge looked at me questioningly. I just shrugged my shoulders and acted as if I didn't have any idea what he was talking about. I then got Mr. Wilkens out of there in a hurry. It wasn't long before others tried to duplicate this, but none ever achieved the perfection of that night.

FLIGHT OF FANCY

Boredom is a cop's worst enemy. More guys have gotten into trouble because they were bored than anything else. I was bored. It was a beautiful Sunday morning. The sun was shining, the sky was blue and there was a gentle warm breeze on the water. I sat on the old pier at the foot of Montford Avenue looking out at the boats passing by. There was the occasional cargo ship from some exotic land bringing their merchandise into port to be unloaded and shipped all over the country. Mostly however, and to my dismay, there were pleasure craft with happy laughing people enjoying the bay. I noticed a helicopter take off from the Inner Harbor area and fly south along the water. About fifteen minutes later it came back north and landed again. I have always enjoyed flying; I'll get in anything that will get me up in the air, so when the helicopter took off again I watched with keen interest. A short time later it returned and landed again. Being the curious sort I  decided to investigate. I drove around until I found the helicopter sitting in an empty parking lot behind the old power plant.

I saw the pilot at the seawall near the helicopter smoking a cigarette. I went over and introduced myself and asked what he was up to. His name was Scott and he was an ex-cop. He explained that he was giving helicopter tours of the harbor. We stood around and talked for a while. There were no customers and since both of us were bored he asked if I would like to go for a ride. I jumped at the chance. Scott took the doors off to allow us to really experience the flight. He fired up the engine and we both buckled our lap belts. Then, with a feeling of exhilaration, up we went. I had only been in a helicopter on one occasion before that so it was all still new and exciting to me. We started south along the water at about five hundred feet.

Within minutes Wagner's Point was slipping below us as we turned east and flew over the Dundalk Marine Terminal. Scott then flew northwest and climbed to about one thousand feet to fly over Fort McHenry. The star shaped fort looked beautiful in the early morning sunlight. The grass was lush and green and set off the red bricks of the fort. I was an avid photographer at the time so I had my camera with me as usual. There were so many things to photograph that I couldn't keep up, nor did I have enough film (this was before the digital age). We continued north into the city flying low over the skyscrapers.

This was a perspective of the city I had never viewed. I was hanging out of the door straining my seat belt to take pictures of some of the architectural details on some of the older building. One of the buildings had a copper roof (which had turned green) and was made to resemble scales (like a dragon's back). On all four corners were gargoyles staring back at me. Suddenly my flights of fancy were rudely interrupted by the voice of my lieutenant over the radio. He wanted to know my location! Now what? Not wanting to lie outright I quickly ran through all of the possible answers. I couldn't think of any rule that said that I couldn't patrol my post from the air. I answered that I was patrolling Boston Street along the waterfront. As I said this Scott turned southeast and headed that way. Of course, with the doors off the noise of the helicopter was very loud over the radio. The LT said that he was on Boston Street and wanted to know *exactly* where I was. By then I could see Boston Street and the LT's car. Resigning myself to the fact that there was no good way out of this situation I stated, "Pull over, get out and look up, I'm right above you." I watched as he did as I instructed. He stood there with his hands on his hips and his hat tilted back. I smiled and waved. He pointed to the open field across the street and motioned for us to land. Not wanting to put Scott in the middle I got on the radio and told the LT that I was going to pick up my car and I would meet him there in ten minutes. He was not happy. After he landed I thanked Scott and bid him farewell. I hurried back to meet with the LT and as I pulled in behind him he got out of his car to meet me. I acted as if it was just another Sunday morning, "Hey LT, beautiful morning isn't it?" I said. He was not amused. I cannot repeat his reply in this forum. I continued my innocent act and asked what I had done that violated the rules.

"At what height does my post end?" I asked as respectfully as possible. He became so flustered he turned red faced and couldn't talk. He turned, got into his car and left. He let me worry for a day or two after that, wondering what action he would take. On the last day I was to work before my days off he called me into his office. When I entered he didn't even look up, he handed me a memo on departmental letterhead and told me to sign it. My stomach turned over, was this an acceptance of disciplinary action or my termination letter? As I read the memo a smile crossed my face. The memo stated in no uncertain terms that from that day onward, no matter where I worked my area extended to no more than 10 feet above the tallest building there.

MARYLAND'S FINEST?

State Troopers in Maryland, as in many states, have a reputation for being "pretty boy" traffic cops. This really hit home for me when I attended a seminar given at Maryland State Police Headquarters. I was talking to a couple of Troopers and they began to compare "war stories". The first Trooper was  bragging about the robbery suspects he had arrested after a high speed chase. Wow, these Troopers do some real police work I thought. He went on to describe how a couple of real bad guys went into a convenience store, put a couple of six packs of beer under their coats and walked out (without paying!). He just happened into the store right after they left and the clerk gave him a description. He jumped in his cruiser and sped off in pursuit. He reached speeds of one hundred mph to catch up with them on Interstate 95 (I-95). After this "chase" he pulled them over and ordered them out of the car at gunpoint where he placed them under arrest. This pretty much proved my original suspicions about them. So, I was not completely taken by surprise by my next encounter.

I was bored again on midnight shift and I was driving the new Pontiac LeMans 400 so I decided to let her loose and see what she could do. It was around three a.m. and I was the only thing moving on the streets.

The stretch of I-95 through Baltimore was nearly completed but not yet open so I jumped on I-95 north and opened it up. In no time I had the speedometer buried and was flying. The Baltimore City Police Department uses portable radios for the most part. These handheld radios do not have the power to transmit more than a few miles. This is fine within the city limits, where there are radio towers and repeaters all over the place. However, once you get a few miles outside the city there is no coverage what-so-ever. Before I knew it I was out of radio range and decided it was time to turn around and head back. I had slowed down to the speed limit (by this time I was traveling on a portion of I-95 that was open although traffic was very light) and was looking for a turnaround point when I noticed a VW van ahead of me drifting toward the grass divide.

It had rained heavily over the past couple of days so the ground was pretty soft. When the left wheels of the van hit the soft shoulder the weight caused them to sink. The sudden pulling and sinking caused the van to roll over and begin flipping end over end. I immediately activated my emergency lights and pulled into the left lane so no other cars would collide with the van if it ended up back on the highway.

It finally came to rest on its roof in the center of the divide (thankfully it hadn't gone into on-coming traffic). I stopped and rushed to the van to render assistance. Several other motorists stopped to help also.

This was in the old days before cell phones were available and as I said my radio was out of range so I asked one of the good Samaritans to drive to the next exit, find a phone and call the Police. "But you are the Police!" he astutely observed. I told him that my radio was not working (leaving out the details, like being way out of my jurisdiction). The VW was occupied by a man with his wife and three small children. I was able to get everyone out and to a safe distance from the van in case of fire or explosion.

As I was administering first aid to the most seriously injured of the five victims a State Police car arrived. The Trooper stopped his cruiser, turned on the emergency lights, put it in park, set the brake, put on his hat, straightened his tie and finally stepped out of his vehicle. At last I have some help with this mess. Wrong, he stepped out of the vehicle into a mud puddle. Being more concerned with his appearance than the victims he got back in his car and began to clean the mud off his shoes! That was too much for me, I ran over to the car and said, "Hey pretty boy if you want to sit in your car while these people are dying at least call for some medical assistance!" I went back to helping the victims and I guess I shamed him to action because he followed me.

As soon as sufficient help arrived I quietly slipped back to the city and my duties. It never fails, whenever you try to get away with something the unexpected happens.

And then there was the Trooper who found out he wasn't Superman. I got a call to the 500 block South Conkling  Street for an assault in progress. When I got there I found a guy sitting on the curb holding his nose. I asked him what happened and he related the following story: "I stopped in the Little Tavern to get some coffee. I parked my new car in front and went in. When I came out there were two guys arguing so I told them to knock it off. When they ignored me I pulled out my badge and said, 'State Trooper, I'm ordering you to cease and desist immediately.' With that one guy took my badge and the other one hit me in the nose. Then they took my gun and drove off in my new car." It didn't take me long to find out who the desperados were and get the Trooper's stuff back. I promised not to report the incident to his department if he promised to stay out of the City.

CAR 54 WHERE ARE YOU?

With the last name of Gordon and the uncanny ability to be the first one on the scene, no matter where the call was, it was inevitable that I would get the nick name "Flash". As this story shows, it is easy to let your reactions outrun your brain.

I was assigned as a backup out of my sector on a burglary call at 3112 O'Donnell Street. As usual I arrived first, in time to  see a guy climb out of the second storey rear window. I yelled for him to stop, but (to no one's surprise) he jumped down into the yard and ran. It's hard to describe the adrenaline rush you get when you are suddenly placed in a possible life or death situation. The body is an amazing creation; we are able to go from a calm restful state to survival mode in a split second. I never was much of a runner but pride is a powerful motivator, I wasn't about to let this guy get away from me. We ran north on Robinson Street and then east in the alley behind Dillon Street. He turned and suddenly jumped a fence into someone's back yard. Baltimore allies are never very well lit so it would be easy to lose this guy in the darkness. He started jumping over fences from yard to yard. I followed in the like manner as best I could wearing street shoes and a ton of equipment. I dodged or tripped over all manner of stuff that people leave in their back yards. We were halfway down the block when I caught him in a yard with a particularly high fence.

After a brief struggle I was able to get him under control and handcuff him. It was at this point that I realized I didn't know where I was or how I was going to get out. He couldn't climb out in handcuffs and if I let him out he would run or fight me again. The primary unit had not arrived yet and it would be useless to try to describe the yard I was in to the dispatcher. I knocked on the door of the house but got no answer. As Oliver Hardy use to say, "This is a fine mess you've gotten me into". How do you get out of this mess without being completely embarrassed and humiliated? If you know, don't tell me because I couldn't figure it out at the time.

I got on the radio and told the whole world (Southeast District anyway) that I had a prisoner and had no idea where I was. I tried to instruct the other units on direction of travel and such but I wasn't really sure myself. After what seemed like hours I saw the flashlight of one of the guys looking for me and directed him to my location. After they got the two of us out of the yard I watched in frustration as they let my prisoner go. It had been a domestic situation and the estranged wife did not want to press charges. Needless to say I took quite a ribbing over that for some time. I can assure you that that was the last time I got myself into a situation where I didn't know where I was (at least while on duty).

THE FAMILY THAT DRINKS TOGETHER...

I'll talk about my biggest and my scariest fights later but for now I'll tell you about my funniest fight. I was dispatched on a call to 1309 South Baylis Street one evening for a family disturbance. This was not an unusual call for that location. I think every time there was nothing good to watch on TV they decided to fight. I was in no hurry to listen to their screaming and nonsense so I took my time and enjoyed the warm summer evening. The sun had just gone down and there was still a touch of red and purple in the clouds.

When I got there I found a husband, wife, and their two adult sons engaged in an argument. As I have observed so many times over the years, they did not begin throwing punches until there was someone there to stop them. The four of them were so drunk that it wasn't much of a fight anyway, but I stepped in and broke them up. I was doing my best "Family Counselor" act to try to settle them down when they decided it was more fun to fight. Once again I stepped in to break it up; only this time one of the punches meant for Dad hit me square on the

 jaw. I immediately changed from family counselor to avenger of justice. I grabbed the son (who had thrown the punch) and started to put handcuffs on him. The rest of the family decided that they were not going to allow me to arrest him. Just like in the Kung Fu movies they charged me - one at a time. They were so drunk and lacking in coordination they couldn't lay a hand on me (when they were trying anyway).

I was like a matador fighting a drunken bull. As each one would charge I would simply step to one side and let them run past me. They ran into each other, parked cars and even the front wall of the house. It was such a funny sight I had to control myself to keep from rolling on the ground laughing. One of the concerned neighbors called the station and said an Officer was

in need of assistance (which I wasn't) so several other units showed up. By the time they got there the whole family was lying on the ground moaning and crying from their various self inflicted wounds. I didn't elaborate on the fight to my colleagues, I just told them I like to go by the old Texas Ranger motto, "One riot one Cop (Ranger)".

THE CHASE

I had only been on the department a short time when my first real car chase occurred. It was about three a.m. and I was working the lower Highlandtown area. We still did not have sirens in most of our cars. I didn't understand it then and I don't understand it now but that's how it was. The cars that did have sirens used the mechanical type like fire engines used.

It was activated by a foot switch on the floor to the left of the brake pedal (I always hated this because I liked to use my left foot on the brake). This particular night I was driving one such vehicle. Anyway, as I was on routine patrol I observe a Ford station wagon operated by a very young male. I get behind him going east on Foster Avenue and turned on my "gum ball machine" (as the single revolving blue light on the roof was lovingly referred to) to pull him over. As soon as I do this he takes off. We quickly accelerate reaching speeds up to sixty mph as we continue on Foster Avenue. He is going through stop signs without even slowing up. I know that some of these as four-way stops so I stay with him through these. However, I'm not about to kill someone or be killed so I slow down at the other stop signs. We fly through the intersections at Potomac Street; Ellwood Avenue and Clinton Street (all four-way stops). When he goes through the intersection at Highland Avenue I slow down to make sure I avoid a collision; this allowed him to gain about a block on me by the time he reaches the intersection at Conkling Street.

At this point he runs a red light and hits another car broadside. Talk about being at the wrong place at the wrong time – its three am and these poor folks enter the intersection just as this maniac runs the light! I can see it coming and, as things like this often do, it seems to be in slow motion. As the cars collide the woman in the passenger side hits her head on the  window breaking it. As I watch the shattered glass falling to the street I see to my horror that the woman's head has fallen with it! As I stop I get on the radio and ask for EMS and assistance for a fatal accident. I am out of my vehicle almost before it stops. I run over to arrest the offender because I have never received first aid instruction on severed heads. I have the young delinquent in cuffs and I reluctantly turn my attention to the accident victims. I can't believe my eyes! The passenger is getting out of the car! It is then I realize that it had been the woman's wig and not her head that came off. You don't know how relieved we both were. Thankfully, no one was seriously hurt in the accident.

It turned out that the thirteen year old boy had "borrowed" his uncle's car for a little joyride. After seeing to the victims I transported my juvenile suspect to the station to charge him. I was just completing the sixth traffic ticket when the Desk Sergeant looked in and the following conversation ensued:

Sgt - "What are you doing?"

Me - "I'm issuing citations for each of the traffic violations this young man committed while eluding a police officer"

Sgt – "You rookies don't know anything do you? He is under sixteen years old and has no driver's license – you have to void all of those tickets (not an easy task back then) and charge him on a Juvenile Custody Report. You better get to it, the uncle is on the way here and the faster you get this kid released to him the better for us all."

This was one of many lessons I learned the hard way – like the time I wrote a four page report and did a thorough investigation on the theft of hub caps from a car. That one got ripped up and thrown at me. I was told in no uncertain terms that my time would be much better spent patrolling the streets to prevent further crime and answering calls than fooling with some petty larceny!

THE LONG HELLO

If there is one thing a cop loves, it's a good high speed chase. There just isn't anything that challenges your skills and gives you a rush like screaming through the streets at one hundred mph trying to out-maneuver your opponent. Times and policy have changed since my days as a beat officer keeping the streets safe for humanity. Today such things are severely restricted (and rightly so). However, let me once again transport you back to the days when the cops were still the good guys and were always right.

It had been fairly quiet for a hot humid summer night. I was patrolling my area, keeping the streets safe when I observed a motorcycle with a passenger on the back without a helmet. As this can be very dangerous if an accident occurred I decided to take action and rescue this young lad from his youthful indiscretion. When I pulled behind the  motorcycle and activated my blue light the driver accelerated in an attempt to escape. A big smile crossed my face.

I had recently been assigned a brand new Pontiac LeMans 400. This was in effect a GTO muscle car without the name. It had the full police pursuit package that included a four hundred cubic inch engine and a four barrel carburetor.

As the Beach Boys aptly put it, "if she had wings man I know she'd fly". If you add to that the fact that it was being driven by the best pursuit driver since Steve McQueen in Bullet the poor guy did not have a chance. I accelerated right along with him. As we wound our way through the streets and alleys the passenger began to reach into his pockets and throw stuff out.

The driver joined in and at one point stuff was coming out like clowns at the circus coming out of a Volkswagen. It was as if their pockets were bottomless pits. After a couple of these objects hit my windshield my suspicions were confirmed, they were disposing of their drugs.

I had decided not to call this pursuit in as some supervisors even back then had a tendency to call them off if there wasn't a felony involved. Since traffic was light and not many people were out I decided it was worth the risk. We continued winding through side streets and alleys at break neck speeds, and on the straight-away we exceeded 100 mph in short spurts. This lasted for about ten minutes but covered less than one square mile. At times I was less than five feet from the back of the bike. I could tell the passenger was getting worried so I backed off just a tad. That was what he had been waiting for, the next time the bike slowed for a turn he jumped off and ran. I wasn't interested in a foot pursuit (they aren't any fun at all) so I continued chasing the bike. Try as he might, he couldn't shake me.

Finally realizing this he decided on desperate measures. The row houses in the area have an opening between them  (some call it a breeze way). He made a sudden turn between parked cars, jumped the curb and accelerated into the breeze way. Unfortunately, he miscalculated the width of his bike which turned out to be about three inches wider than the opening. He succeeded in wedging the bike in and in the process trapping himself. The ceiling was only a few inches above his head and his leg was stuck between the wall and the bike. It took the Fire Department Rescue Squad an hour to get him free and out of the breeze way. After all of that I still found drugs in his pockets that he had missed in his efforts to discard the evidence.

CAR STOP BLUES

I have always despised drunk drivers, even before it was popular and fashionable. Early one mild March evening I was driving eastbound on Eastern Avenue when I observed an old Ford F150 pickup truck in front of me weaving and crossing the center line. I activated my blue light to pull him over (still no sirens) but he refused to stop. Traffic coming in the opposite direction was too heavy for me to get around him so I continued trying to pull him over for about a half a mile with no success. Finally we reached the area where Eastern Avenue opens into four lanes in front of City Hospital. At this point I passed him and cut in front of him to make the stop. As I walked back to the pickup I could see that this guy was a classic redneck, and a big one too.

When I asked him for his license and registration he began to fumble in his wallet, dropping it on the floor. I decided this guy is too drunk to even understand what's going on so I  ordered him out of the truck to conduct my field sobriety tests. He refused to exit the vehicle insisting he had done nothing wrong. After it became obvious that talking was not going to get this guy out, I opened the door, grabbed his arm and pulled. Well, I may just as well have tried to lift the truck, this guy didn't budge. I planted my feet against the truck and pulled with both hands, same result. Now I was getting a bit angry (and embarrassed) so I tried a couple of the pressure points I learned in the Academy (see, what did I tell you in the introduction – when all else fails go back to your training), still he didn't budge. I would have felt silly calling for a back up unit because this guy wasn't fighting me he just wouldn't move. I decided to call for the patty wagon and let the wagon man help me.

The wagon arrived driven by good old John Schoff. John was a kindly veteran officer who had been on the job forever. He was always helpful to the poor ignorant rookies and I knew I could depend on him for a quick resolution to this sticky situation. He asks where my prisoner is and I tell him he's in the truck. "You know you are supposed to arrest them and cuff them before you call for the wagon don't you?" He asks. I sheepishly explain my problem to which John replies, "HAHAHA! Rookies! Let me show you how it's done." John, who is smaller than me walks up to the truck and in his meanest, gruffest voice says, "Get out of the truck you're under arrest!" "Nay say I constable, nary shall I submit to your oppression! (of course criminals don't talk like this but I am uncertain of the sensibilities of my readers so I have taken poetic license). I can see John's neck turn red so I know this guy is in trouble now. I watch John go through the same routine I just went through trying to pull this guy out, to no avail. "Alright, enough of this nonsense" says John, "I'll go on the other side and push, you grab him from this side and pull."

He goes to the passenger side and we begin our concerted effort. The guy is like the Rock of Gibraltar, still no result. In his anger John pulls out his mace and sprays the suspect.

Of course mace can't tell the good guys from the bad guys so I end up getting more of it than the suspect. About the only thing the mace does to this guy is make him angry. He comes out of the truck in a rage and I'm the closest object for him to unleash it upon. Unfortunately, the mace has had more of an effect on me than on him and I am unable to see what I'm doing. As this guy and I wrestle each other and fall to the street John comes around and starts hitting the guy with his night stick (no fancy Academy defense tactics for old John). Once again, I receive as much punishment as the suspect. Finally, somehow, we get the guy handcuffed and into the wagon.

I ended up spending the next couple of hours in the emergency room getting the mace washed out of my eyes and my lacerations bandaged up. Afterward I asked John how he ever survived on the job this long, surely not every cop he has beaten up is as forgiving as I.

FATHER MURPHY

One of the most difficult tasks for a young officer is the responsibility of being the Officer-In-Charge (OIC). The prospect of working with your squad one day, supervising the next, and then back to working with them again is daunting. It was especially difficult for me as I had only two years on the street when I was given the responsibility of supervising a squad with an average of ten years experience. I give a lot of credit to the members of the squad for not stuffing me in a dumpster somewhere. With that background I'll relate the story of the first sticky situation I had to handle as an OIC.

I was in the home stretch of a Saturday night on the four p.m. to midnight shift. Just when I thought I had gotten through it without incident I got a call to meet 234 car (Bob) at the church in the 200 block of South Conkling Street. He didn't say what he wanted but I could tell by the tone of his voice it wasn't a social call. When I arrived Bob had a juvenile in handcuffs in the back of his patrol car. As soon as I got out of my car the kid started screaming, "Are you the boss? This stupid pig shot at me for no reason!" In his usual civic minded manner Bob told the kid to shut the #$%#@ up or he would throw him in the trunk. I asked Bob what had happened and he informed me he had been flagged down by a citizen who told him someone was trying to break into the church.

He checked and found an open window, however it was too small for him to enter. Not certain if this was a burglary or simply a window left open Bob went to the Rectory and got the Monsignor to come to the church to check it out. When they went inside they surprised the kid, who then jumped out of the window and ran. Bob initiated pursuit of the suspect with his gun drawn (this was a felony suspect and Bob had no way of knowing what to expect). As they rounded the side of the church Bob yelled for the suspect to stop or he would shoot. This produced no results and the chase continued. When they reached a fence in the back of the church the suspect vaulted over it with no trouble at all. When Bob tried to stop he fell on some loose gravel and his weapon discharged. The suspect, hearing the shot stopped immediately and was captured. This was a street wise kid who had been in trouble before. He knew our rules  better than some of our own did. He knew, as Bob did, that warning shots were strictly prohibited by the Department, so naturally he surmised that Bob had been shooting at him. I wasn't sure I believed Bob's account of the events.

For one thing there was no dirt on his pants from his fall. However, I resisted the temptation to jump to conclusions and started my investigation.

My first concern was where the shot had actually gone. Had it gone into the ground, the suspect, or some innocent bystander? Despite an exhaustive search I wasn't able to find it. I noticed that there was very little chance that anyone could  have witnessed what had transpired back there. I could tell that Bob knew I didn't completely buy his story. After my initial investigation I decided (right or wrong) that I would write Bob out of this one. "So, is this where you slipped in the dirt and fell causing your weapon to discharge?" I asked. It took a minute to sink in that I was going along with his story, then he got a very relieved look on his face and said, "Yeah, that's where it happened." I made some scuff marks in the dirt near the fence and then to add to the validity of the story I told Bob to get on his knees in the position he was in when his weapon discharged (and of course get his pants dirty). Then I went back and took a statement from the Monsignor, informing him of the findings of my investigation. He gave me a knowing look and a smile and thanked Bob and me for a job well done.

The next day I was called into the District Commander's office to discuss the incident. He was holding my justification report and I could see the anger on his face. He started the conversation by asking, "Do I look like some kind of %#@&*% moron?"

I knew then I was in trouble. My answer of course was that he in fact did not resemble any moron I had ever seen. He went on to tell me in no uncertain terms that he knew my report was a crock and I better come clean if I wanted to keep my job. I held my resolve, my career flashing before my eyes. Just when I was sure all was lost he got a phone call. Within a few seconds I knew it was Father Murphy. Being a good Catholic boy my Commander showed proper deference to the Priest and as the conversation progressed I knew I was going to be okay. After the initial pleasantries the only words out of his mouth were "Yes Monsignor" and "Thank you Monsignor". It was great to see him on the other side of the table for a change. When he got off the phone he told me that the Monsignor wished to commend us for a job well done and that he hoped the officer who had fallen was not injured. He smiled and said, "Okay son you won this one. The next time you won't have the church to back you up." "You never know" I replied as I walked out of his office triumphantly.

THE GIANT & THE PINBALL MACHINE

I've always had a little cowboy blood in my veins, that's why I always got excited when I got a call for a good knock down drag out bar fight. Of course, in my mind they were always like the ones in the Westerns I had watched as a kid. The punches, bottles broken over the head and smashed chairs never resulted in any serious injury. As I gained more experience and reality set in I learned to dread them.

On a cold winter night in February 1976 I got one such call to the bar at Highland Avenue and Baltimore Street. Always  the first on the scene and never one to wait for my back-up to arrive, I charge through the front door of the bar to find the biggest man I had ever laid eyes on. This, in and of itself, would have given pause to any sane human being. To make it even more interesting he is holding a full size pinball machine over his head ready to throw it over the bar. At a quick glance I see several guys scattered about the floor like rag dolls. Most seemed unconscious; a couple of them are trying to crawl away from this angry giant. Time seemed to stand still as we faced each other just six feet apart. The only sound was a beer bottle still spinning around on the floor. I could tell that he was enjoying himself and was fully prepared to take on this cop without a second thought.

I look at the night stick in my hand and then my eyes went to the pinball machine still held over his head. My nightstick suddenly looks very small. Looking me straight in the eye with a big grin on his face he broke the silence, "Okay cop, what are *you* going to do?" I knew what I was going to do, everyone in the bar knew what I was going to do, but I had to stand up to this guy and *tell* him what I was going to do, "I'm going to the hospital, maybe we can get adjoining beds." With that his grin turns to a smile, and the smile turns to a laugh. He turns away and drops the pinball machine and then turns back to me. Still laughing he puts his hands behind his back and says, "You got cojones Officer, go ahead and take me in." I am more than happy and very relieved to oblige him. Looking about as we wait for the patty wagon I can see that he had done considerable damage to the bar. There are at least six guys that need to go to the hospital. I later found out that my giant had four arrests for assault & resisting arrest on his record. Nobody believed he gave up to me (the rookie) without a fight. I decided from that point on that I would use my brains and humor first only resorting to force as a last resort. That philosophy worked well for me throughout my career.

This particular bar had the distinction of being the location of my run in with the biggest man I ever saw and a few years later the largest fight I was ever in.

I responded to a call for a Signal Thirteen (officer needs assistance). When I arrived there were at least a hundred people in the street, most of them fighting.

Before it was over we had Officers and patty wagons from four districts. I made nine arrests which filled one wagon, and it took another five wagons to transport the remainder of the prisoners. I never did find out what started it. None of the people I arrested knew why they were fighting; they had just joined in the fracas.

TOUGH LOVE

I never would have dreamed that there was a tribe of Indians living right there in southeast Baltimore. No there  weren't any teepees or buffalo, but there was a lot of counting coup (striking your enemy, usually with a club) and scalping. Back then I thought they were called the Lumbees because they lived on Lombard Street, however since then I have broadened my interests and discovered that the Lumbees are primarily in North Carolina and are the largest Indian tribe east of the Mississippi. This tribe had its own ideas about which laws to obey and which to ignore. The lack of respect for the domestic violence laws meant that if you did get a call for a domestic it would be a doozy.

Early one morning in late December of 1977 I was dispatched on just such a call. The only information we had was that there was a domestic disturbance at a specific address on Lombard Street and the caller wished to remain anonymous. As my backup and I approached the door we could hear the shouting and breaking of glass. Our knocks either went unheard or ignored. Suddenly the boom of a shotgun rang out followed by the piercing scream of the woman. We both hit the door at the same time knocking it off of its hinges.

The man was standing in the living room holding a double barrel shotgun. He had it broken open and was about to reload. The woman was lying on the floor bleeding profusely from what was left of her legs. I grabbed the shotgun from the man's hands as my partner grabbed him around the body to control him. He began to fight and pulled away from my partner's grip. The fight was on. As we knocked each other back and forth across the room the woman was screaming, not from pain but at us for hurting her man. I had let the shotgun go (as it was empty and I didn't see it as a threat). While we were trying to handcuff the man I noticed that the woman had retrieved it and was trying to load it. All the while she was yelling for us to leave her man alone, that she was wrong and he had the right to "discipline" her. Apparently the sound of the shotgun blast had prompted additional 9-1-1 calls as several other officers arrived on the scene. We were able to get the suspect handcuffed and begin first aid on the woman, as she cursed and spit at us. Even though we charged the man with Assault with intent to Murder he was never tried. They both swore that we were lying and that he was cleaning the shotgun when it accidentally went off. She spent the rest of her life in a wheel chair as a result of her wounds.

GAY BARS & NIGHT STICKS

I have mentioned my complete lack of worldly experience when I joined the department. Please keep this in mind as you observe my lack of discretion in terminology and my complete shock at the response thereto. Also please keep in mind that in the 1970's people were not as in-your-face with alternative life styles.

I received a call out of my Sector for a disorderly crowd at a bar in the 2500 block of Boston Street. This was an area as yet unfamiliar to me. It was a busy Saturday night so I was on my own, which didn't bother me because I was still invincible back then. As I turned right off of Lindwood Avenue I noticed an immediate change. I went from a residential neighborhood full of row houses with marble steps into an industrial waterfront full of dirty aging warehouses. This part of Boston Street was still cobblestones with train tracks running up the center of the street. The street lights were significantly fewer adding to the dark dirty feel of the area. As I drew closer to the 2500 block I could see the lights of two night clubs that were adjacent to each other; the only signs of life in an industrial area this time of night.

As I pull up in front of the bar I observe a very large crowd in front yelling and causing quite a disturbance. I notice that there is something very different about this crowd.

 First there are no women, what kind of night club would attract a bunch of guys without dates? Second, most of the guys were better dressed than the typical Highlandtown bar crowd. Their talk and mannerisms were definitely *not* those of the steel workers I was used to dealing with. I had never seen such a thing. I exit my patrol car and walk over to the crowd and in my most official voice inform them that they must cease and desist and relocate their activity immediately.

I am not too surprised when most of them ignore me because they could not hear me over the din and had not as yet seen me. I decide to work my way to the center and focus on the apparent instigators sheltered within. Immediately, I notice a powerful odor emanating from the crowd, is that perfume? After much pushing and shoving, I finally reach the two guys arguing in the center and I tell them to knock it off. They too ignored me. I give them the benefit of the doubt. Maybe in the heat of their argument they did not recognize my omnipresence. I walk between them and holding my night stick in front of the

face of the larger of the two I yell, "If you don't knock it off I'm going to put this stick so far up your butt you'll have to swallow to get it out!" Now, that's intimidation for you. I am totally unprepared for what happens next.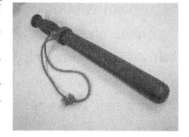

He smiles at me, takes the end of the stick between his thumb and forefinger and begins to suck on it! He looks me in the eye and says, "Oh sweetie, that's the best offer I've had all night."

Okay, stop right here and put yourself in my place. What are you going to do? You have forty people surrounding you who are whooping, hollering and laughing at you. This citizen has embarrassed the heck out of you but hasn't really violated any laws yet. Pretty tough situation, huh?

So, there I stand wanting to pound this guy into the pavement but knowing I can't do it. Then, to add insult to embarrassment, the guy puts his arms around me and tries to kiss me. This is the break I was hoping for (don't get the wrong idea now). He has just assaulted a Police Officer. Everyone knows you can't assault a Police Officer and get away with it. I parry his advance and grab him by the arm and inform him he is under arrest. He pulls away and begins to run, cheered on by the crowd. I immediately give chase having adopted the Royal Canadian Mounted Police slogan (we always get our man, uh woman, uh whatever!). I decide right away that I am going to do this without any help, after all, how could I get on the radio and announce that I am in foot pursuit of a stick sucker? The guy is pretty fast and after three or four blocks he is starting to pull away.

I realize that I am failing as a Mounty (if I only had a horse), so in a last ditch effort I try a trick I had seen work in the movies. I stop and throw my stick at his legs to trip him up and bring this nightmare to an end. As soon as I let go of it I know its fruitless (throwing the stick I mean). It bounces twice and comes to rest against the wheel of a car. The stick sucker runs back, picks it up and runs off with it! I went back to the area every night for a month hoping he would return so I would have the opportunity to regain my honor. Alas, it was not to be. However, we would be reunited (my nightstick and I) a few years later, but that is another story.

SCARED STRAIGHT

If you drive through the 2400 block of Boston Street today it's hard to picture the way it was in the 1970's. Thanks to urban reclamation Boston Street is now a beautiful tree lined

boulevard with luxury town homes and condos on the west side and remodeled warehouses containing a variety of businesses across the street. The only clue left to the old Boston Street is contained in the median. If you look closely you'll see the old cobblestones that used to make up the street are now just accents. Where expensive town homes and finger piers with luxury boats now stand there was nothing but vacant lots over-grown with weeds and one dilapidated wooden pier (both pictures in this story were taken from the same vantage point thirty years apart). The train tracks ran right down the middle of the street in the early 1970's. The trains still brought raw materials to the can manufacturers and left with the finished products that eventually contained food shipped all over the world. I can't even remember the number of times Boston Street was closed due to one of the trains derailing. It was never anything serious; it just came off the tracks and dug into the street and blocked traffic until they could get it righted. I remember several incidents that occurred along this stretch of waterfront. I've included a couple of them in these pages.

For years the only thing there was a "ghost ship". That changed briefly one spring when "Big" Paul (not to be confused with "Tall" Paul) got the bright idea that he could dock his boat there for free and have it close to home to boot. Big Paul as his name should tell you was a pretty big guy. Standing six feet tall he  weighed about three hundred and fifty pounds, most of which was in the upper body. He owned and operated Big Paul's Bar on Eastern Ave. The police were never called there by the establishment for anything. Big Paul handled his own problems. I arrested him once and I had to use leg irons on his wrists because handcuffs wouldn't fit. Ah, but that's another story.

Anyway, being a good cop I kept up with who owned what and where, so when I drove past and noticed a young boy on the boat alone I figured I'd better investigate. It was still early spring and a bit too chilly to be boating.

There was no way to get my car down there and, with nothing but open fields, surprise was out of the question. I walked carefully, avoiding the larger areas of weeds and growth and trying not to fall through the rotting boards of the pier. Paul's boat was a cabin cruiser of about thirty feet in length. It was not new but appeared to have been well maintained. I started wondering how Paul could afford such luxuries out of his income from a corner bar.

That thought remained in the back of my mind until I had the chance to look into it a few years later when I was working in the Vice Squad.

By the time I walked down to the boat this kid had two or three minutes to hide whatever he was doing but had nowhere to run. As I approached the side of the boat a young blond haired boy of thirteen or fourteen years old, wearing jeans and a blue sweater came over and said, "Hi, can I help you?" I asked what he was doing and he said he was looking for something he left on his dad's boat. I asked him who his dad was and he said John Rogers. I told him I found that very interesting since this boat did not belong to someone named Rogers. I then went aboard, keeping the lad in front of me and noticed some obvious signs of forced entry. He tried to explain that someone had broken into the boat last week and his dad knew all about it. He was a very brazen young man.

Apparently Big Paul had someone watching the boat for him, and although the kid went undetected, I did not. Big Paul's Cadillac slid to a halt behind my patrol car and he rushed down the pier to the boat red faced and out of breath. This normally menacing giant was even more so in this condition. The kid, being from the neighborhood, knew Paul (and his reputation) immediately. He turned pale as he started to apologize to Paul for breaking into his boat. After a quick inventory Paul told me there were four pieces of electronic equipment missing. Turning to the boy he asked where they went.

When the boy refused to answer, Paul looked at me and winked so the kid couldn't see and said, "Okay Officer, just forget about it, I don't want to press charges. Leave the kid with me, I'll handle this." All of the color drained from the kid's face as he contemplated his fate. In an instant he jumped over the side into the water. Neither of us was prepared for that. After all, that water was oily, murky and cold. I started to worry when the kid didn't surface. After about a minute I started to take off my equipment to go in after him. I was certain by now he must be drowning. Just then he broke the surface holding a piece of electronic equipment over his head. He tossed it up to me and before I could order him out of the water he dove again. This went on, despite my objections, until all four pieces of equipment had been recovered. We then pulled the kid out of the water and Paul gave him some towels to dry off. Paul was so impressed with the gumption of this kid that he decided not to press charges. Once we got him somewhat dry I took him home to explain what had happened to his parents. I was pleased with their reaction when I was finished the account of events. In so many cases the parents want to blame someone else (like the police) when their child gets into trouble. Not in this case. They made the youngster apologize to me and later that day they took him around to see Paul. I never had another moment of trouble out of that kid; I guess he got "scared straight".

DOLLARS TO DONUTS

I was on the midnight shift one very quiet November night in 1976. By now I had almost eighteen months on the street so I was a veteran cop (in my own mind). I had "tried up" (checked the physical security of) every business, stopped every suspicious car, and written every parking ticket I could write. I stopped by the bakery around three thirty a.m. and watched them baking bread and donuts for the coming business day. This was one of my regular stops on midnight shift. The baker, Kevin was an interesting guy. I enjoyed the aroma of fresh baked bread and confections and watching him mix the ingredients in a large commercial mixer and end up with these amazing tasty treats. Being a good cop I left with a bag of donuts and filled buns to see me through the night.

By four a.m. I am getting *really* bored so I decide to have some fun. I search the "holes" until I find one of my colleagues (Bob) resting his eyes behind a warehouse. I park behind the warehouse and approach his vehicle in a stealthy manner on foot. The hubcaps on the 1976 Dodge police vehicles we were driving had holes around the edge. As quietly as I can I slide several firecrackers into the driver's side rear hubcap. Once they are lit I duck behind the building to watch the fun. When they go off they send his hubcap rolling across the lot with a horrendous noise.

Bob jumps up, hits his head on the roof, flips on his lights and rolls out of the car. I was doubled over with laughter. Hearing me he goes into a rage and begins to chase me. I jump into my car and take off with Bob in hot pursuit!

I lead him on a merry chase through the industrial area which is of course, deserted at this time of the morning. The chase begins like a Hollywood movie with me racing through puddles, around heavy equipment and between buildings. We travel around a couple more warehouses and then turn north onto Janney Street for a couple of blocks and then go west on Lombard Street. Once out of the industrial area the streets are much better, making travel easier. With absolutely no one else on the street I exceed the speed limit by a reasonable amount (by reasonable I mean I weigh wrecking the car against Bob catching me and exacting revenge). After turning north on Haven Street for a couple of blocks I end up coming out onto Pulaski Highway with Bob still on my tail.

This calls for drastic measures, Bob isn't giving up and I know how he is when he is mad. I make a quick right into the Holiday Inn parking lot, shoot past the office to the back of the building, do a Hollywood 180 degree turn and speed back toward the exit. This particular Holiday Inn had a covered drive near the office so people could check in without being exposed to the elements.

The other lane ran parallel with a small median between the two. I stay to the right passing under the covered portion and Bob is approaching me on the left. As I draw abreast of the office Bob is coming toward me.

My window is already down as it was a fairly warm night for November so just as we pass I throw a cream filled bun striking his windshield dead center, scattering cream everywhere. He comes to a screeching halt, throws it in reverse and the chase resumes. I turn eastbound on Pulaski Highway and accelerate in an effort to shake him. We are about six blocks away when a call comes over the radio for a holdup alarm at the Holiday Inn 3600 Pulaski Highway. We both turn around and respond code three. As we stop and exit our vehicles the manager runs over to us and shouts, "What the devil was that about? I had two guys in here with guns in my face, you guys show up like the Calvary to save me, and then you turn around and leave!" Needless to say that was a tough one to explain, (especially the creamed car) talk about embarrassing moments!

I had one more evening of "fun" before I gave up on firecrackers. I saw Tom sitting in his vehicle in Patterson Park just after the bars had closed. It had been a busy shift so far, running from call to call. Bob had stopped to catch his breath but was still keyed up from all the action.

I pulled the some fuses out of the firecrackers and as I pulled next to him I lit it and threw it into his car. As it flew past his face I took off. In a totally unexpected reaction he bailed out of his car (to avoid the "explosion") and just stood there as it did not happen. I turned around and returned to rub it in a bit. As I pulled up laughing Tom calmly pulled his mace from his belt and shot me square in the face! Now it was his turn to laugh as I bailed out of my car choking and coughing while trying to wipe the mace from my face. Of course the more I rubbed the more I spread it around and the worse it got. There was a water fountain nearby and I made my way to it to wash my face. This provided some relief but I was still having a rough time of it. Tom, realizing that the "joke" had gone too far loaded me into his car and drove me to City Hospital where the kind Emergency Room nurses administered first aid and cleansed the offending chemical from my eyes. Neither Tom nor I ever mentioned the details of this incident to anyone – the police "code of silence" reigned supreme!

THE STANDOFF

We were not really given much training on hostage/barricade situations when I was in the Academy in 1974. Back then it was the Marine Corps "take the hill at all costs" mentality. Having only been on the 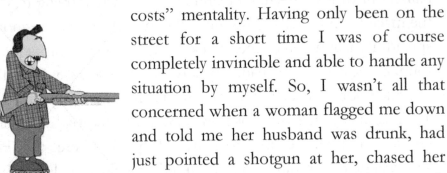street for a short time I was of course completely invincible and able to handle any situation by myself. So, I wasn't all that concerned when a woman flagged me down and told me her husband was drunk, had just pointed a shotgun at her, chased her from the house and swore he would shoot anyone who entered. I had enough experience to question her about any additional firearms in the house (he had a single barrel twelve gauge shotgun in his hand, and an entire collection of rifles in the basement). I got a good idea of the layout of the house and as I approached I could see the man moving around on the second floor. I did my best Hollywood cop imitation and entered the first floor. At this point my plan was to keep the man from the weapons in the basement and the beer in the kitchen. I figured I could talk him into giving up and even if I couldn't I had reduced the threat by several magnitudes.

Some of you may wonder at this point why I did not call in the SWAT team for this. Let me give you a bit of history on how things were done at the time.

There were still some very radical groups active in this country in 1975. The Symbionese Liberation Army (SLA) the Weather Underground and Black Panthers had strained the ability of standard police tactics. All police cars started using locking gas caps after several cars were destroyed by placing lighted rags in them. Across the country police were being set up and ambushed. As a result SWAT (Special Weapons and Tactics) was born. These units used military-style light weapons and specialized tactics in high-risk operations that fall outside of the abilities of regular, uniformed police. The Baltimore SWAT teams began forming in 1974/75 when the Tactical Unit realized a need for better training and better equipment to handle riots, and hostage situations. Following in the footsteps of other agencies they were going to name their team SWAT but the department found the word SWAT to be too harsh so Baltimore developed their Quick Response Team (QRT). An impressive name for a unit with a modest start. The reader must keep in mind there was nothing quick about the response in those days. The department could not afford to have a team or teams of highly trained officers sitting around waiting for something to happen. All of the QRT members had regular duties and were "called up" when the need arose. I had been assigned to block traffic on Kresson Street a couple of months prior to this for a man holding his wife hostage. I was there for three hours until the QRT arrived. In addition to that a lone armed subject inside his own house was not considered outside the responsibilities of the plain old beat cop.

This was a typical Baltimore row house where you entered the living room and the stairs were open on the side and located in the dining room. The kitchen was at the back of the house as were the stairs to the basement. The second floor had the master bedroom in the front a bathroom at the top of the stairs with two smaller bedrooms at the back of the house.

I stood in the dining room off to the side of the stairs so he couldn't get a shot at me and called up to the man informing him that I was a Police Officer and ordering him to throw down his gun. He began to yell and as his speech was very slurred I couldn't understand anything but "*kill you!*" He then starts down the stairs. I am in no hurry to shoot the guy so I begin yelling,

"Stop and throw down you gun" as I am retreating into the kitchen. He comes halfway down the stairs, sees my gun pointing at him from the kitchen and runs back up the stairs. I then run to my previous position in the dining room and again order him to drop the shotgun. At that he yells and starts down the stairs again. I retreat to the kitchen again, yelling for him to drop the gun. This goes on for several minutes until I start to laugh, I feel like I am in a cartoon. Finally I tire of looking and acting like a cartoon character so I decide to take action. This time when he comes down the stairs I don't retreat, I reach up and grab his ankle and pull him down the stairs.

He lands in a heap at the foot of the stairs and I retrieve his shotgun before he can pick it up. My adrenalin is up and I am ready for a fight, but he just lays there and begins to cry as drunks often do, about how nobody understands him. There are times you really wish you had a video camera!

My aversion to calling the QRT team manifested itself in a rather humorous way on another occasion. After receiving a call for a burglar alarm at Epstein's Department store on Eastern Avenue I discovered that a back door had been forced. I called for a  K-9 unit to search the building. There were generally two or three K-9 teams on each shift for just such circumstances. Unfortunately on this particular night there were none available. I then requested a backup unit from my squad to assist me in searching this huge building. My old buddy John responded and we entered the building to search. We soon realized the futility of the two of us searching this building alone with a potentially armed suspect inside with virtually unlimited places to hide and ambush us. This was another of those situations where some would request assistance from QRT. John had no more desire to be stuck there all night than I did so we hatched a plan. We yelled that we were sending in the K9 and then John started to bark like a dog. The guy gave up – he had been bitten before!

A HELPING HAND

It was a quiet shift change Sunday morning in June of 1977. After working a very busy four p.m. to midnight shift on Saturday and only getting four hours sleep on the quick change over I was ready for a nice easy day. I already know what you're  thinking; he wouldn't be writing this if he had a nice easy day. Okay, stop thinking ahead and keep reading. Around nine a.m. I get a call to the 300 block of South Ellwood Avenue for a suspicious person. The houses on South Ellwood Avenue all face the upper part of Patterson Park and have a very nice view of the city skyline in the distance. I have never received a call to any of the houses on this stretch of Ellwood Avenue before. As I respond I wonder what someone would have to do in Patterson Park on a Sunday morning to be suspicious. As I pull up to the intersection of Ellwood and Bank Street there is no one on the street. I can see the entire park from this vantage point and there is nothing more suspicious than some people walking their dogs. Ah! Maybe that's it, maybe one of those dogs is planning something, or maybe it doesn't have the proper papers! Well, I will have to leave that to the dog police, I wouldn't want to infringe on their territory. I am just chuckling to myself over these crazy thoughts when a man approaches and tells me he just saw a guy carrying a rifle and peeking in the window of a nearby house. The guy then crawled through the rear window (okay that does seem a little suspicious).

Now, this is a job for the real Police! I exit my vehicle and approach the house while calling for a back-up unit. I hear shouting coming from inside the house as I cautiously approach from the blind side and creep up to a  side door. Inside I can hear a woman crying and pleading and a man threatening in an agitated manner. I can tell by his voice that the guy is out of control. He is just inside the door I am next to and I can see movement through the curtains. What should I do? Do I rush in, surprise the guy and take him down? What if the door is locked? He will surely hear me turning the knob and then possibly shoot through the door or shoot the woman. I don't want this to turn into a long drawn out hostage situation because I really don't think this guy can be reasoned with (and you already know my feelings on QRT from previous incidents). Just as these thoughts are going through my mind I hear the siren of my backup units approaching (I failed to mention that each sector had one car with a siren – it was usually designated as a two man shotgun car). I know I have to do something quickly, but what? This guy is out of control and not thinking clearly. I put my back to the wall on the same side of the door as the knob and shout, "Hey man the cops are coming you better take off!" Just as I hoped, the guy doesn't wonder who is yelling, he only thinks about escape. I hear him shout to the woman that he will be back another time to finish this, and out the door he runs.

As the barrel of his rifle comes out the door I grab it and pull it from his hands at the same time sticking my foot out to trip him. He hits the ground hard and I am on him cuffing him before he knows what hit him.

As it turned out, no one was hurt. The guy had been stalking this woman for weeks but she hadn't reported it (this was before stalking laws). In a strange way I got my wish. Although I had to put up with five minutes of excitement, I spent the rest of the morning quietly doing paperwork!

COWBOYS & COPS

There was a bar in the 400 block of South Conkling Street called *Slim Brows*. Now, what made Slim's unusual was that it was a Country bar. Highlandtown had a bar on nearly every corner back in the 1970's. Most were just small establishments that catered to the steelworkers and autoworkers who liked a couple of beers before going home from work. The larger bars were "rocker" bars with some even having pole dancers (in case you are wondering, I do have a pole dancer story). So, being the only Country bar in the area Slim's drew an entirely different clientele. Many of these guys had come north to find work; most were true "rednecks" (and I use that term in a respectful way). Anyway, Slim's is larger than your average neighborhood bar. As you walk in the front door there are a dozen or so tables arranged so that they can be moved to create a dance floor. The bar stretched the full length of the room along the left side. As with most bars the lighting is subdued and in this case there are numerous cowboy pictures and paraphernalia hanging on the walls.

It was inevitable, mix country music, alcohol and rednecks and you *will* have a bar fight. One hot summer night the call came out for an altercation (translation – bar fight) at Slim's. Being a young gung-ho officer I arrive first and rush in to restore order (backup? I don't need no stinking backup!).

Before my eyes can even fully adjust to the low light level a chair hits the wall right next to my head. I have never seen anything like it in my life. It looks like a movie fight scene. There must be thirty people throwing punches, bottles, chairs, anything that isn't nailed down (Yippy ky yo ki ya! Buckaroo).

How in the world am I going to break this up? How am I going to keep from getting myself broken up? It doesn't seem as if my uniform has impressed anybody very much. Just then six guys come toward me in a group.  Oh boy, I'm thinking, I'm in for a real fight now! As they get close they all turned their backs to me and surround me. The biggest of the lot yells out, *"Anybody touches the cop is a dead man!"* My first emotion is relief! I'm not going to get the stuffing kicked out of me after all. My next emotion is embarrassment as four of my fellow officers come running in to assist me and I am "hiding" behind a bunch of civilians! It was a good feeling to know there are people out there that will look out for you but I took a lot of ribbing over that for a long time.

LOOK BEFORE YOU LEAP

The 2800 block of Boston Street is now upscale homes and shops. In the 1970's however, it was an industrial area full of old, dark, dingy warehouses. There was one of these warehouses in particular where the alarm went off almost every  night. It became very tedious responding and searching this huge building so often. After the first few times the owner even refused to respond. You can imagine how I felt when early one Sunday I was driving by and noticed an open window on the side of the building. The alarm had not gone off but it would be possible to gain entry (the window was about five feet off the ground) so I parked my car just under the window and called for the "night reference" (owner or his representative). After waiting nearly an hour I get hungry so I open my lunch and begin eating. My lunch in those lean years was usually a cheese sandwich and some pretzels (convenient but not exactly exciting). I am about halfway finished when I'm startled by a loud bang as a bag lands on the hood of my patrol car. This is followed by three more large canvas bags which were obviously very heavy judging by the noise they make on impact. As I jump out of the car to investigate the source of these airborne bags I see someone backing out of the window.

He lowers himself down to the hood of my car before he realizes I'm there (look before you leap had never occurred to him). I grab him, pulled him off the car and handcuff him without resistance. I can tell he is very upset about being caught. He tells me that he has been the one setting the alarm off all of those times to wear me down so I would get sloppy and stop checking the building. Another instance of excellent, diligent police work (also known as dumb luck). The owner is so happy with my excellent police work that he writes a letter of commendation to my District Commander. In reality I think he is just elated with the prospect of not getting calls all hours of the night about his alarm!

THE EYES HAVE IT

I always found it very interesting working the waterfront area of Canton; I never knew what to expect with so many merchant marine sailors and stevedores running around. On February 3, 1976 I was working 236 Post, patrolling the waterfront when I got a call to meet the Police Boat (Intrepid) at the foot of Clinton Street to be transported to a British ship at anchor off the Dundalk Marine terminal.

That was the extent of the information they gave me. What in the world was a Baltimore City Police Officer going to do on a British ship? I was soon to find out. It was a cold, blustery winter evening, not fit for man nor beast to be on the water. I have never been much of a seaman so I was a bit apprehensive. I met the Intrepid in the designated location and, with some  difficulty was able to get aboard. I was then informed by the Sergeant that there had been a serious stabbing on board the British ship and that its captain had requested police to assist. The journey to the *Alisa* across the dark, choppy water seamed to last for hours. With each passing minute my imagination was running wild. I had never been on a seagoing ship before. Did they have their own security force or would I be going this alone? When we finally reached the ship our reception did little to quell my fears. The Intrepid came along side and ran into the aluminum gang-way in the process.

A gruff looking sailor who resembled the pirates I used to see in old movies yelled down to us, *"Watch the #%*#@$ gang way you moron, where did you learn to drive a boat anyway?"* After much hesitation and gnashing of teeth I was able to get onto the gang-way without falling in the water or being keel-hauled by the pirate. Once aboard (alone) I watched the Intrepid slowly  motoring away taking with her any chance of backup. The Sergeant informed me on the radio that they had another call and would be back for me when they were done. I was truly and completely alone.

The sailor with the foul mouth turned out to be the Captain (Christopher C. Mahon) and the only person on board who spoke English (the crew being all Chinese). He informed me that there had been a "bit of a row" (British word for a disturbance or argument) over a card game and one of the "chinks' had cut another one pretty badly. He informed me that there had apparently been some question about cheating that led to an altercation. The victim (Lan Tai Fain) was getting the best of the fight using Kung Fu to his advantage against his opponent (Wong Chee). The suspect, not wishing to lose face (and the fight) pulled a knife and stabbed the victim several times.

The Captain upon hearing of the stabbing rushed in and broke it up. I asked to see the victim and as we headed to their infirmary I also inquired as to the location of the suspect. I was told that the suspect had fled with the knife to parts unknown 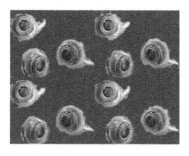 on the ship, *"If he's left the ship your worries are over mate, he's drown by now."* On our way to the infirmary we passed the crime scene. It was the strangest sight I had ever seen. The room was only about 8' by 8' with a small table and six chairs in it. There was blood on the walls and on the floor was a large pool of blood, which was not unexpected. What I was not prepared for was the twenty or so eyes staring back at me from the blood! The Captain could see the puzzled (and sick) look on my face. He explained that fish eyes were the snack of choice among the crew. The "snacks" had been knocked off the table and ended up in the blood. Judging by the amount of blood I was pretty sure the victim was no longer with us. This was confirmed when I reached the infirmary. The ships "doctor" informed me that he had died from a severed artery.

I was in no hurry to search a ship that size alone for a suspect that didn't even speak English. I postponed that task by interviewing the witnesses (through the Captain of course). When I could no longer put it off I asked the Captain to accompany me on the search. He too was reluctant but had no choice. We worked our way down into the bowels of the ship until we were in a section where I was unable to stand upright due to the pipes and such.

The scene reminded me of one of those places in the movies that are dimly lit and have monsters of every sort lurking in the shadows. Just then my monster appeared from the steam and shadows shouting something in Chinese and waving the bloody knife. Perfect! Now my movie was complete. I drew my service weapon and ordered him to drop the knife (in English of course as I am not conversant in Chinese). He continued to slowly advance shouting in Chinese. The Captain yelled back at him in Chinese and about the time my finger was tightening on the trigger he dropped the knife and slumped to the floor crying.

I handcuffed him and recovered the knife. We worked our way topside where I found two Homicide Detectives and three back-up units waiting for me. The guys from the *Intrepid* had been unable to raise me on the radio so they had brought reinforcements. A little late I might add. Anyway, being young and naive I didn't protest when the Homicide Detective told me to stay and guard the crime scene while they took my prisoner downtown. Okay, you guessed it; he took credit for the arrest, got the commendation for bravery, and got to go to Hong Kong for the trial. I got seasick and nauseous from fish eyes. I learned my lesson, the next fish eye caper I get I'm keeping a close eye on the suspect, even if I have to pick up a few extra eyes to help me out.

LOVE CONQUERS ALL (ALMOST)

It was a warm, pleasant evening in early August of 1977. I was working the four p.m. to midnight shift in Canton. Canton got its name from the can manufacturing factories in the area. For many years this area of Baltimore supplied cans to most of the country. Those factories are now condominiums and upscale businesses. They had already started to decline by the 1970's but they were still a major employer in the area.

I wasn't thinking of cans that night as I drove east on Fleet Street and noticed a motorcycle westbound "pop a wheelie". I turned around and stopped it in the 2400 block. The teenage driver was very apologetic and respectful so I decided to give him a break. I told him to take the bike home and not bring it out again that night (I know - you're thinking, "He doesn't have the right to do that". You are correct; however I considered this a gentleman's agreement rather than an abuse of authority). A few hours later I was cruising slowly in the 2400 block of Fait Avenue. This is a typical city street in a residential neighborhood; there are two lanes of traffic with cars parked on each side of the street. As I came nose to nose with a transit bus traveling in the opposite direction a motorcycle pulled into my lane and accelerated to pass the bus. Obviously the driver had not seen me. In the blink of an eye he struck my cruiser head on, rolled onto my hood, over the roof, off the trunk and hit the ground.

I was sure this was a bad one; the kid had to be dead or in serious condition after a head-on collision like that. I was calling for EMS as I exited my vehicle. As I got back to the cyclist and bent down I recognized him from my earlier encounter. To my relief and amazement he got up and began to brush himself off!

I noticed a large dent in the top of the gas tank on the motorcycle that had not been there earlier in the evening. When I saw the young man in obvious pain and holding his groin I knew what had caused the dent. When I asked him why he had been in such a hurry he replied he was late picking up his girlfriend. My response was, *"Well, she isn't going to have any use for you in your condition!"*

So far I have included a couple of stories about motorcyclists who made some bad choices. It would not be fair to exclude a situation where your protagonist displayed a less than stellar motorcycle performance.

The Baltimore Police Department was ever on the watch for new and innovative ways to protect the citizens of our fair city. With this in mind a new program was instituted that placed small easily maneuverable motorcycles in each district to seek out crime and criminals in areas not easily reached by car. The department purchased twenty small Honda motorcycles and had them painted and striped as Police vehicles (no sirens though).

Of course you cannot just give a cop a motorcycle and tell him to go catch the bad guys.

There was a training course set up at Druid Hill Park to be taught by Officer Lenny Petrovich. This assignment was taken very seriously by Lenny and he said he would not put up with any foolishness (was that a challenge?).

I had been riding a motorcycle since I was sixteen (my first vehicle was a Triumph Bonneville 650cc) so I did not expect to learn much in a two day course. The first day consisted mostly of the vision the department had for the program, tactics we were expected to use and all applicable laws. The second day we got to ride. We started off going through cones and practicing basic riding skills. By lunch time everyone felt they had it down pretty well. It was at that point that Lenny decided to show off some of his skills. He looked at his assembled class and said, "Don't any of you knuckle heads try this!" He then accelerated up a steep hill as fast as the bike

would go. Upon cresting the hill both wheels left the ground in an "Evil Knievel" type stunt. It all looked great until he hit the ground. The bike came out from under him and he slid across the grass before coming to a stop next to a tree. Guess what happened next. That's right; everyone wanted to prove they could best the instructor. One after another tried it and in each case the result was the same. Finally I could take it no longer; I had to show these guys how it was done. I accelerated up the hill, left the ground and sailed to a perfect landing. I turned around to gloat on my achievement and ran right into a tree! Fortunately I did little damage to the bike and I only got a few scrapes and bruises.

Lenny swore us all to secrecy and gave us our new Departmental Motorcycle license. Although I enjoyed the class and the two day reprieve from my daily routine it was all for naught. Before I even got the chance to use the bike in my district some hot shot wrecked it. I don't believe any of the twenty survived the month. So much for good intentions.

BAD HAIR DAY

When I joined the department in 1974 I was a long haired, bearded motorcycle riding "hippy" college student. The day before I started the job I had to cut my hair, shave and refine my liberal attitude. I spent the next three years trying to get into a unit where I could grow my hair and beard again. My break came in May of 1978 when I was assigned to the Vice Unit. At the time the Southeast District had a Vice/Narcotics Unit. It consisted of two Sergeants and four Detectives. Vice was  responsible for those issues of moral turpitude (prostitution, gambling, underage drinking, etc) while the narcotics guys concentrated on illegal drug trafficking and sales. The Vice guys had the best gig by far. Each month we received an envelope of cash from HQ to spend undercover (translated – bar bills). We concentrated on the bars in Fells Point for the most part. The small neighborhood bars rarely gave us any problems (with the exception of some small time gambling on the horse races at Pimlico). The variety of bars in Fells Point gave us something new to look at every night. We would go from live folk music one night to Disco Inferno the next (that's right – Disco).

My partner, "Spanky" was everything his nick name implied, a little rascal. Up to that point in my career I had not met anyone on the job who was so crazy (I've met a few since though).

On my first night in Vice, Spanky and our Sergeant "Rocky", who was a throw-back to the 1950's, went to Fells Point to do some vice enforcement. We went from bar to bar looking for under-age drinkers, prostitutes, gambling, you know, all those things that the Bible warned us about. Needless to say we had to fit in so at each bar we would drink a beer while we were checking things out. I couldn't believe it; I was getting paid for this! After the eighth or ninth bar we were walking across Broadway when Rocky spotted a hooker hitch hiking. He told me to go over and see if I could get her to solicit me so I could arrest her. I looked him in the eye and said I couldn't do it. "Sure you can, just walk over and start talking to her and get her to offer sex for money." he said. "I know *how* to do it" I replied, "but this curb is too high. I can't lift my foot high enough to get over it." Rocky and Spanky doubled over laughing; they had the kid too drunk to walk!

With that as my introduction to the Vice Squad I decided to work some cases that didn't require so much drinking. I got a tip that a guy was making book (illegal gambling) and selling drugs out of his beauty parlor on Eastern Avenue. After weeks of surveillance and placing some bets myself, I obtained a search warrant for both the shop and his home.

Having determined his schedule I decided that we would execute the warrant late on Saturday night when the shop was closed and he had the most money. We hit the house first.

It was a dark, moonless night. There was just enough light from the single streetlight halfway down the alley to allow us to navigate the obstacles in the yard and get to the house without using flashlights. I placed a uniform officer at the front door and myself and three other Vice officers planned to go in through the second floor rear window. I knew the suspect had his office in that room and it was easy to climb up on the porch roof and go in through the window. Once all three of us were on the roof I quietly tried the window but it was locked. Spanky pushed me aside and hit the window frame with a ten pound mall as he yelled, "Police, search warrant". He went in first and I heard a grunt. I went in next stepping down, as Spanky had onto the sofa which was right beneath the window. As I stepped down I again heard the grunt. Turning back toward the window I saw the third officer come in and step down exactly as Spanky and I had. It was then that I noticed that there was a guy sleeping on the sofa! As the third officer stepped on his chest he let out another grunt and then rolled over and began to snore! The strangeness of the place struck us immediately. There were candles and incense burning all over the apartment. In the center of the room was a huge statue of an erect penis. Lying on the floor in a circle were four guys completely naked. We had smashed through the window as they were in the middle of a little orgy. My first thought was, "Oh my goodness it's true what they say about hair dressers!"

When we had all of the occupants rounded up (there was no need to frisk them) I noticed that the guy who had been on the sofa had a familiar face. As I was trying to remember where I had seen him I glanced over to the end table next to where he had been and low and behold, my old nightstick!

So this was the guy I had been hoping to run into for years. I asked him if the night stick belonged to him and he said it did. I decided to let him keep it, after all I had no idea where it had been or how it had been used. What, with all of the drug charges he was facing I  didn't need to go into court and explain how he was in possession of my property!

We conducted our search and seizure as quickly as possible but we were still forced to endure flirtations and propositions that made my skin crawl. Once we finished the house we executed the warrant at the beauty shop.

We had found enough to make our case against the hair dresser for gambling as well as for the drugs we found in the apartment. The irony of it was that it turned out to be my wife's hair dresser. She had an appointment that Monday with him. When she came home she was in the middle of telling me about these nasty bully cops who had broken into the hair dresser's house for no reason when I broke up laughing. She realized then that she was talking about me and broke up too. I told her I didn't think it was a good idea for her to go back to him because if he realized she was married to me he would probably shave her bald.

I mentioned at the start that we had it better in Vice than the Narcotics guys. I could relate some tragic stories I was involved in to substantiate this but I'm trying to keep this on the lighter side so instead I'll relate a story that was pretty funny for all but the unfortunate guy it happened to. I have no qualms about relating my various adventures, however as I do not wish to embarrass this gentleman I will call him only Burt.

After a lengthy investigation that included many hours of surveillance, controlled buys and interrogations of arrests the Narc guys finally had everything they needed to obtain a search warrant for a house that was involved in major drug trafficking. All of the detectives involved met for a pre-raid planning session to minimize mistakes and confusion (some, in their haste had done things like hit the wrong house). Confident that they were ready they gathered their gear and arranged to meet the uniformed officers a couple of blocks away. Little did they know that they had missed one important detail. Maybe, if one of the detectives had covered the back of the house and seen numerous large piles in the yard it would have clicked that they were in for more than they bargained for. The uniformed cop assigned the task however paid it little attention.

Drug dealers do some pretty radical things to protect their operation. This particular dealer had a vicious Pit Bull Terrier. This in itself was not uncommon; however in this case he had had its vocal cords cut so that it could not bark. As a result the unsuspecting detectives hit the front door and rushed right into this vicious monster. Before it could even register on his brain the dog attacked Burt. It sunk its teeth into his right upper thigh just below the groin and would not let go.

Burt (who was originally from Puerto Rico and had a distinct accent) began to scream, *"EYEEEEEEE, the dog, the dog — get the dog!"* as he hopped around trying to extricate himself. One of the guys tried to pull the dog off but was having no success so Burt pulled his service weapon (a puny thirty-eight caliber snub nose revolver in those days) and tried to kill the dog.

On his second shot he again let out a scream, *"EYEEEEEEE, my foot, I shot my foot!"* It was impossible not to laugh and at the same time dive for cover as Burt emptied his revolver at the dog. Of course as soon as the shots rang out the officer covering the back called in an "Assist an Officer — Shots Fired" and the entire district descended on the house. Finally, the dying dog was pried from Burt's leg and order was restored out of pandemonium.

Despite Burt almost being turned into a eunuch or having his femoral artery severed the raid was a success. A major drug operation was put out of business (even if temporarily) and justice was served. For some reason Burt did not care for dogs much after that.

HANDCUFFS & HUSTLERS

I was having the time of my life working Vice in the Southeast District. The only part of it I didn't care for was going after the male prostitutes along Eastern Avenue; most of which were fourteen to seventeen years old. We normally used a van to pick them up. One of us would drive and the other would hide under a blanket in the back until the "code word" was used. At that point the driver would pull over and the other guy would jump out from under the blanket and yell "Police!" This had worked pretty well for a week or so while my new partner Roy drove (Spanky had gotten a transfer to the big leagues at HQ by this time). That changed when it became my turn. Roy knew I was nervous about picking up boys, job or no, it made me very uncomfortable. As I drove down Eastern Avenue near Linwood Avenue I saw a young boy hitch-hiking. I pulled over and asked where he was going. *"Where ever you want to go and whatever you want to do"* was the answer. I told him to get in and I began to drive. As I was trying to get the kid to offer sex for money (the only way to get a soliciting conviction) the kid pulls out a knife and puts it to my throat! This is perfect, I think, we caught ourselves the kid who has been robbing all of these older men in the area. I am able to work the "code word" into my response to his demands for my wallet, and nothing happens. Out of the corner of my eye I can see the blanket moving slightly but Roy is not coming to the rescue. Then I realize the movement is him laughing! He doesn't know I have a knife to my throat; he is getting his kicks making me deal with this kid on my own.

Now I'm angry, and a little bit concerned. If I try to alert Roy the kid may cut my throat and bail out before he can get out from under the blanket. My only option is to get the knife from the kid on my own. I use the old trick of looking behind him and saying, *"Hey, what's that!"* He turns for a second to look and I grab his knife hand and a struggle begins. For a kid he is pretty strong and I realize I may not be able to get the knife away and control the vehicle at the same time. As calmly as I can I say, *"Roy, the kid has a knife, can I get some help up here?"* I see Roy peek out from under the blanket thinking that I'm joking. When he sees the knife his eyes get big and he starts to get up and scramble to pull his gun. Of course he gets all caught up in the blanket and ends up falling over kicking and tearing at the blanket. The kid sees this and then, letting go of the knife, he bails out and runs as I bring the van to a stop. I help Roy out of the blanket, chastising him the whole time and then we start chasing the kid. After a couple of blocks we catch up to him and make the arrest. He ended up confessing to eleven armed robberies in the area. He also gave us information on two of his friends who were doing the same thing.

A couple of nights later I was working alone when I saw the two suspects standing on the corner of Eastern and Montford Avenue. I pulled over and walked up to them. I identified myself as a cop and both of them started to run. I was fast enough to grab the first one in a couple of steps. I quickly threw him in the car and handcuffed him to the steering wheel (after I removed the keys). I then took off after the other one. With the head start he had I couldn't catch him so I walked back to the car.

As I got in and took out my keys I remembered that I had taken my handcuff key off the ring for an undercover operation so I wouldn't give myself away. Now here I was with a kid handcuffed to my steering wheel and no way to drive or release him. It was pretty embarrassing having to call for a unit to meet me with a key. That was the subject of some jokes for awhile. Anyway, this kid went for (confessed to) several robberies also and we made the city safe for old men to pick up young boys again.

WHEN YOU GOTTA GO...

The Fells Point area is one of the oldest areas of Baltimore city, dating back to the original shipping port of the 1700's. Many of the old buildings have been restored and now contain shops, restaurants, and bars (lots and lots of bars). It's odd how the area developed along cultural lines. In the 1970's the bars on the east side of Broadway were mostly owned by Greeks catering to the blue collar crowd and sailors, and on the  west side were those who catered to a "yuppie" crowd. There were colorful names like *The Acropolis; The Horse You Rode In On; Wharf Rat; Dudas* and *The Cat's Eye Pub*. We would battle our behinds off on the Greek side and then have to hear the "I pay your salary, who do you think you're talking to" line on the yuppie side. I always preferred the Greek side myself. The area was becoming very trendy in the Seventies so we were getting many more professional people moving in. One of those was U.S. Senator Barbara Mikulski who bought a row house in the 700 block of South Ann Street. Ms Mikulski is a reasonable but demanding person (and a former Catholic Nun). She understood that we couldn't be everywhere (even when her house was burglarized) and for the most part she sympathized with our plight. However, when she walked out her front door one evening with an out of town visitor and two guys were relieving themselves on her front steps she lost it.

She called the District Commander at home and told him in no uncertain terms that he was to get this *serious problem* under control. The next day the order went out concentrating all of the District's resources in the Fells Point area to eliminate the "pisser" problem. I was still in Vice at the time and my partner and I were no longer to be evaluated by our gambling or prostitution arrests, it was now based on the number of "pissers" we caught. I'll never forget one poor guy (a Greek merchant marine) who walked around the corner from the bar he had been in. The bar was packed so I suppose it was pretty tough to get to the men's room. Being Greek, and a first time visitor to the United States, I suppose he didn't understand how serious a crime he was committing. When he unzipped and began to urinate on the wall of the building he was hit by the full weight and force of the BPD. My partner and I were on foot and having noticed the violation we were swooping in for the kill. At the same time there were two marked radio cars driving by in opposite directions. The first officer saw the guy, screeched to a halt, bailed out and started running toward the offender. The second officer didn't see the guy but he saw the other officer needing assistance so he screeched to a halt, drew his weapon and joined in the chase. At the same time a car full of detectives that were passing by on their way to a raid observed the excitement and joined in.

We all reached the suspect at the same instant. The poor guy, who hadn't seen any of us coming, was suddenly grabbed by two uniformed and six plain clothes officers. He was so startled he didn't even think to stop and zip up.

He was spun around and handcuffed before anyone realized he was still urinating. We all looked down and began jumping back to avoid the stream. One of the detectives got his pants leg soaked and began hopping around and cursing. My partner and I were laughing so hard we had tears in our eyes. I turned to the officer who still had his gun in his hand and told him to holster it up. "While you are at it why don't you holster your prisoner up as well?" I asked. The look on both the suspect's and the cop's face was hilarious. No one wanted to help the poor guy put his private parts away so we had to un-cuff him and let him zip up before he was put into the wagon and transported to the District. I can just imaging the story as it passed around the merchant marine, "You better watch your weenie in Baltimore!"

MONKEY BUSINESS

In March 1979 I was temporarily assigned to Criminal Investigation Division (CID) Narcotics to help with a case of stolen drugs at City Hospital. Since security was tight we were pretty sure it was an inside job. The hospital administrator set us up in a supply closet across from the drug storage cabinet. We had a camera set up on the drugs with the monitor in the supply closet. It only took a couple of days to identify the villain and make an arrest. All in all it was a pretty routine operation. What makes it stand out as worthy of inclusion in my work of literary genius was the aftermath.

I got some of the hospital letterhead and forged a letter from the hospital administrator to the Lieutenant. It went something like this:

Dear Lieutenant:

I regret to inform you of a serious indiscretion which resulted from your surveillance operation in my hospital. I had my security staff do a complete inventory of the supply closet prior to turning it over to your officers. Once the operation was over I again had an inventory done. It is my sad duty to inform you that a substantial amount of hospital property is missing from that supply closet. I have included the complete list and request that you take appropriate action to have the items returned.

MISSING ITEMS:

200	Pencils - City Hospital embossed on same
25	Writing tablets - City Hospital embossed
1000	Small paper clips
2	Rhesus Macaques
1	Gross of red rubber bands

Your assistance in this matter will be appreciated.

Sincerely,
Will Hurlbutt
Hospital Administrator

If you knew the Lieutenant, you would already be rolling with laughter. He was one of the shakiest bosses I ever worked for. He worried about everything. He swore we would get him fired before he could reach retirement. When he got this letter he went nuts! He ranted and raved, claimed it was a conspiracy against him.

He got everyone who had been on the case into his office. With beads of sweat on his forehead he read the letter to us. I was the only one who knew it was a hoax. You can imagine the indignation on the part of the other officers.

Denials flew everywhere. The Lieutenant listened with growing agitation.

Finally he said he had no choice but to turn it over to the Internal Investigations Division. At that point I decided to bring  this little game to an end. I spoke up and asked if he knew what a rhesus macaque was. He had no idea so he pulled out a dictionary and looked it up. "It's a monkey!" he exclaimed. So I asked why they would have two monkeys in a supply closet and how would someone sneak them out. Suddenly everyone started speaking at once. No one had seen any monkeys in that closet. Why would anyone steal two monkeys? It was complete chaos until the Lieutenant looked at me and let out a roar, "YOU, this was your handiwork wasn't it?" I could contain myself no longer. I laughed so hard I was in tears. Suddenly, that office was not a safe place for me to be. I ran out just ahead of shouts, kicks and flying objects. For months after I heard monkey sounds every time the LT walked through the building.

In my never ending quest to cause ulcers in my Lieutenants I pulled another heartless prank on another of my bosses a few years later.

The push for urban renewal was at its peak at the time. Everyone wanted to live downtown all of a sudden. As a result old row houses that had been rentals to the poor were being bought, gutted and remodeled into show places the original occupants could only dream of. The new Police Commissioner decided that it would be politically advantageous and convenient to make just such a move. He bought two houses on Scott Street and was having them gutted and combined into one luxury townhouse. The district was made aware of this and special attention was given to the property. As the remodel was nearly complete an alarm system was installed.

One pleasant Sunday morning in early June the alarm was set off. One of my officers responded and I went to back him up. He arrived a couple of minutes before I did and was coming out of the house when I got there. He informed me that the Commissioner's wife and son had come to inspect the progress and had forgotten about the alarm. We bid them adieu and went on our way.

That was when an evil plan hatched in my twisted mind. I called for the LT and he stated he was in the station so I went to his office. I mustered up my best worried look and started my story:

"You will probably be getting a call from the Commissioner so I thought I'd prepare you." He immediately lost all color in his face.

"Why, what happened, I heard the call for Scott Street."

"Well, you know what a hot head Joe can be; he arrived and saw a young black male inside the house. He drew down on him, ordered him to the floor and cuffed him. About then a woman came running down the stairs yelling at him so he threw her to the floor also. That's when I arrived and recognized that it was the Commissioner's wife and son. We got them up and brushed them off but I don't think they are very happy about the whole thing."

He just sat there, his mouth open and his face pale and perspiring. I watched his expression as his career flashed before his eyes and then I said,

"Only kidding! All's well. We had a nice chat and left them at the house looking around".

I cannot repeat the response that was forthcoming. I will say that I learned some new profanity that morning. Inexplicably every request I submitted for vacation days for the next six months were denied. Not only that, but there were a few "Needs Improvement" boxes checked on my next performance evaluation for some reason.

This seems like a good place to add a short incident involving me, the Three Stooges and the Police Commissioner.

You may have seen pictures from an old episode of the Three Stooges where they were in police uniforms (if you haven't seen it I've included it below).

I purchased a framed copy and hung it on the wall in my office at HQ. One day, while in a particularly mischievous mood I made up name tags and pasted them onto their uniforms. On Moe I placed E.V. Woods (then Police Commissioner). On the other two I placed the names of two of his Deputy Commissioners. Everyone who came to my office got a chuckle out of it (my boss pretended he didn't notice).

As time went by and the novelty wore off I didn't give it any more thought. One day I am sitting at my desk when Commissioner Woods stops by for a visit (the first and only time I was visited by a Commissioner). He just walks in, sits down and starts asking how things are going as if we are long lost pals. As the conversation progresses I see him looking around the room at my wall hangings.

At the time I had a very nice collection of police patches mounted on one wall. Suddenly it hits me that his name is on  the Stooges picture. I start to sweat a bit and hope he isn't a Three Stooges fan. Wrong! He sees the picture, laughs and walks over for a closer look. As he approaches I state that I hope he has a sense of humor. Commissioner Woods is the guy who always let you know he would not hesitate to demote you if you disappointed him. He turns from the picture, looks at me and says, "I think it's funny but I'm not sure those guys will, you should probably take the names off." With that he walks out and I collapse in my chair.

Once I recover I walk over to take the names off and notice my good fortune. The names of the two Deputy Commissioners are there plain as day, however the name tag for the Commissioner had fallen off! Thank goodness for cheap glue!

ANOTHER FINE MESS...

Image; It's all about image and perception. As a street cop you have rare occasion to interact with the "elite" detectives from the Criminal Investigation Division (CID). As I have related in a previous story I had already found at least two of them in the Homicide Unit to be less than ethical. I was about to meet a couple more.

I was on routine patrol along the waterfront on Boston Street in the early morning hours in August 1980. As I slowly cruised the streets, I enjoyed the balmy summer weather. It was so much better working the midnight shift when things (both  the weather and the citizens) had cooled down. Now that the bars had closed and the streets were empty, I decided to stop at the *Sip & Bite* for a sip. The *Sip & Bite* was an all night dinner that served the kind of meals that you had to be intoxicated to appreciate. When I entered there were a few couples seated in the booths. There was one guy standing at the counter. As I approached the counter, I noticed what appeared to be blood on his hands and shirt. When he saw me looking, he bolted for the front door. While it is not illegal to run, even in the early morning hours, and it is not even illegal to run away when you see a cop, it is, however very suspicious. My curiosity was peaked. I gave chase. It was a very short and uneventful chase. I didn't even have time to radio in that I was in foot pursuit.

As he ran out the door and turned left to run east on Boston Street he collided with a street light pole. Already somewhat inebriated and now dazed from his sudden introduction to a light pole, he just lay there on the sidewalk holding his head.

I did a quick frisk for weapons of mass destruction (namely mine) and then asked him what he was doing. Contrary to the myth perpetrated by Hollywood, a cop does not read someone their rights every time they question them. There has to be a crime (that you are aware of) and the person has to be a suspect. At this point, all I knew was that this guy had blood on him and he didn't like cops. The answer to my question came slowly. First, he began to shake, and then cry. Then, between sobs, in halting gasps he said, "I think I killed him." "Who and where" I asked. He informed me that it was his drinking buddy and that he had left him on some dead-end street a few blocks away. I searched him again, more carefully this time and then handcuffed him and placed him in the back of my car. I instructed him to direct me to his friend. Within a couple of blocks, he pointed down Lakewood Avenue. I turned and about halfway down the block I saw a man lying in the street. I exited my vehicle and checked on the man. He was in fact dead from multiple stab wounds. I got on the radio and requested an ambo (we were not medically trained to pronounce a person dead not matter how obvious) and a Homicide unit.

After the ambo arrived and officially pronounced the subject dead and I had a couple of backup units to protect the crime scene, I started my investigation. I knew that a confession from an intoxicated person would  not hold up in court. A person has to be sober to waive their constitutional rights. So, rather than ask direct questions about the crime I asked some general questions to help fill in the timeline. I asked such things as where he lived, where he had been that evening and how he wound up on a dead-end street in Canton. The key fact that I gleaned from this was that he had a truck and that he had left it parked around the corner near the *Sip & Bite*.

I took the keys and while I was still awaiting the arrival of the Crime Lab and Homicide detectives, I went in search of the truck. It didn't take long to locate. As I shined my flashlight into it, there on the dash was a bloody knife. I double-checked that the truck was locked (so that it would not be tampered with) and returned to the crime scene.

The Crime Lab arrived and began processing the scene. A short time later the elite Homicide detectives arrived. I filled them in on what I had learned and handed the keys to the truck over to them. I was told to take the suspect to the Homicide Unit at HQ and begin my report. My quiet, peaceful night had turned into a paperwork nightmare. I filled out forms and reports for the next several hours.

All-in-all though I felt pretty good. I had caught a murderer, not something a patrol officer got to do very often (even in a city with three hundred murders a year). I went home that morning feeling as if I had made a difference. The feeling didn't last long. I should have learned from my last encounter with these guys. I hadn't. The next night at work I saw the report where Homicide had made an arrest and cleared the murder on Lakewood Avenue. Okay, no matter who got the stat I could still feel good about getting a murderer off the streets. That was not to be either. The elite detectives had bungled the case. They had gone to the truck and recovered the murder weapon (without a search warrant or having the Crime Lab process it). They had questioned the suspect without a lawyer and while he was still intoxicated. The case was thrown out at the preliminary hearing. I still get angry even now when I think about it. That ended my respect for the elite detectives of CID.

WISHING ON A STAR

Midnight shifts were always a challenge after three a.m., especially in the winter months. Once you have checked all of your businesses and there is no one left on the streets it is very boring. I still remember those seemingly endless nights of riding the streets and not seeing another living soul. The city was so peaceful then. There is an old saying, "Be careful what you wish for, you just might get it." Apparently my side partner (Mike) had never heard this one. We were sitting on the lot at  Aliceanna and Washington Streets talking to pass the time and stay awake. Mike was starting to worry about me because I kept "seeing things". Actually, we were having a meteor shower; every time I would see one and tell him to look it was gone. I was seeing one every few minutes and he had yet to see one. Anyway, Mike says, "It sure is quiet; I wish we would get a good call, like a naked woman or something." You guessed it, a couple of minutes later I get a call to Lakewood and Hudson Streets to investigate the trouble, a man has a naked woman in his van. Mike and I look each other and start to laugh. He gets on the radio and volunteers to back me up and off we go.

When we arrive at the location, a guy gets out of a conversion van (these were popular at the time – they were basically vans that were converted into mini-motor homes with a bed in the back) and approaches me explaining that he had met a girl in the bar and started buying her drinks.

They were getting along pretty well so he invited her over to his place. She agreed, but after they were on the way she said she had to stop and pick her son up at the baby sitter's house. He didn't care for the idea but he didn't have much choice. After they picked up the five year old boy the woman put him in the back of the van and told him to go to sleep.

He was reluctant to go by himself so she crawled in the back with him. Then, she started to take off her clothes. Once naked she lay down with her son and went to sleep (or passed out). "What was I suppose to do then?" the guy asked. "I was afraid to wake her up because I thought she might accuse me of undressing her."

I tell him to turn the interior light on so she can see the uniforms and not be frightened, and then I lightly shake her. I have to shake her several times until she finally wakes up. She looks at me, and then notices that she is naked and begins to scream. She becomes frantic, accusing me or raping her. She tries to kick me; forcing me to retreat from the van (I have a rule about fighting naked women). Unfortunately, we have no female police officers on our shift so calling for reinforcements would have been useless.

Mike and I continue to reassure her that she has not been raped and doing our best to calm her down. We are finally able to talk her into getting dressed and letting us take her home.

I am sure she was going to make a complaint against me to Internal Affairs, and although I am innocent and have witnesses, an accusation of rape is not something I want on my record. It turned out that she didn't make a complaint, but I was on edge for a couple of weeks. From that point on I told Mike to leave me out of his "wishing on stars".

THE HANGING MAN

Handling a suicide was always emotionally draining. To witness the total despair and lack of hope on the part of the victim and the devastation it brings to the family always makes one reflect on one's own life. Police, of course can find humor in any situation (it's a defense mechanism of course) and while some may not see the humor in this story it was hilarious (and an emotional release) when it happened.

I received a call to 225 South Clinton Street for a suicide, meet the victim's daughter. When I arrived I found a young woman in her early twenties sitting on the front steps crying. She told me that her father had been distraught lately and that she had come over to check on him. When she entered the house she found him dead, hanging from the kitchen light fixture. When I entered the house it was very dimly lit. Strong sunlight was coming in through the kitchen window backlighting the victim who was hanging just inside the kitchen door. The rope had stretched so that his feet were touching the floor. I called for the Medical Examiner and was in the kitchen starting my report when Sergeant Bill Staley came by to see what I had. While I was briefing him on the situation Officer Tom came by. He walked right up to the kitchen door and started talking. Not realizing that the guy "standing" in the doorway was actually the victim he said, "Excuse me" expecting the person to move out of the way.

He continued to talk, his face showing the obvious frustration that this ignorant person would not get out of his way. He tried once again to be polite but of course the guy still didn't move.

Finally in frustration he said, "Come on pal get the heck out of my way will ya?" and he gave him a light shove. With that the victim began to swing and the body turned toward Tom so he could see his face. Startled, Tom jumped and started running backward. He fell over a chair, got up, and continued moving backward knocking furniture over like he'd seen a ghost. As he literally ran from the house, the Sergeant and I were laughing so hard we had to sit down. From that day forward when someone wanted to get Tom's goat there would make some reference by word or gesture to the Clinton Street swinger.

STREET JUSTICE

Domestic violence is a hot topic these days, with all kinds of support groups and aggressive new laws. In 1980 things were a bit different. There were no ex-parte orders and if the abused didn't testify the case was thrown out of court. If anything was going to change an abusive spouse it was the cop on the beat. That brings me to the story of the Lindsey's. Outwardly they appeared to be an average family in Canton, husband, wife and three  young children. It wasn't long before I found their dark secret. Tom Lindsey was an auto worker at GM. After a hard day on the line he would stop and have a few beers on the way home. Once he got home his favorite recreation was to knock the wife around a bit to show her who was boss.

My introduction to this came when I was driving past the house one evening on routine patrol. As it was a lovely spring evening everyone had their windows open and I had the windows of my patrol car down. As I passed 2512 Foster Avenue I heard a woman screaming and a man shouting. I stopped to investigate and on locating the source I knocked on the door. Mr. Lindsey came to the door with fury in his eyes in an agitated state. When he saw the uniform the transformation was amazing. He became polite and friendly, inviting me in for some iced tea. Although I didn't want the tea I did want to get inside the house so I accepted. Once inside I saw Mrs. Lindsey drying her face and straightening her hair.

Tom yelled for her in typical Archie Bunker fashion to get us some iced tea and be quick about it. When Joan came back with the tea I asked her if she was alright. Her words said yes, and she even tried to smile, but I could see the frightened puppy look in her eyes. After finishing my tea and being assured by Tom that it had only been a little argument I went back to patrolling my post.

A couple of days later I saw Joan and the three kids walking to the grocery store. I stopped to talk with her about Tom. The conversation went something like this:

"Hi Joan, hi kids, beautiful day isn't it?"
"Oh yes, I love days like this."
"How's Tom doing?"
"Okay."
"Tom has a pretty bad temper doesn't he?"
"Only with me."
"Does he ever hit the kids?"
"Occasionally. But only if they won't listen to him."
"How often does Tom beat you?"
"A couple of times a week, depending on his mood."
"Why don't you call the Police and have him arrested?"
"Then what? He gets back out and beats me worse than ever."
"Don't be there when he gets out."
"Where am I going to go with three kids? I don't have any family and I can't find a job without skills."

So it went, we've heard the story a thousand times before. I went to the neighbors and talked to them asking them to call the Police any time they heard things heat up at the Lindsey's.

Over the next couple of weeks I got several calls and with each one Tom got bolder and cockier. He knew Joan wasn't going to press charges and he knew without her I couldn't do a thing to him. One Saturday night I got another call for a domestic.

When I arrived I found Joan bleeding from the knees, hands and head. I asked her what he had done and she said he had thrown her through the front door, down the marble steps onto the sidewalk. I knew the answer already but I had to ask if she would press charges. Of course the answer was no. Tom came to the door yelling for me to get away from his house or he would make a complaint of harassment. He was sick and tired of me always hassling him. Well, as Popeye says, enough is enough and I'd had too much. I walked up the steps, opened the door and walked into the house.

I grabbed Tom by the ear I pulled him into the dining room where we could have some privacy. I then reached down to the case on his belt and pulled the knife he always carried ("for use at work"). I opened it, cut myself on the back of my hand and then dropped the knife. I then put my hand on my gun and said, "Tom, assaulting an Officer with a deadly weapon could get you twenty years in jail, but more than likely it will get your fool head blown off. So here's the plan. If you ever raise a hand in anger to your wife or kids again you can kiss your sorry butt goodbye." With that I let go of my gun, marched him to the front door, and threw him through it to the sidewalk. As I was letting go I said, *"Okay big man, let's see how you handle someone your own size."*

When he jumped up yelling I arrested him for disorderly conduct on a public street. As we were waiting for the wagon I told Joan that Tom and I had come to an understanding and that I would be stopping by unannounced to check on them. I can almost hear some of you screaming "Police brutality!" Not to confuse occupations here but sometimes you have to fight fire with fire.

I don't know if Tom and Joan lived happily ever after, all I know is that I never again heard of Tom letting his temper get out of control with his family.

DON'T GET MAD...

There is an old saying, "Don't get mad, get even." I took that advice in one particular case I was working in 1980. There had been a couple of burglaries in the Washington Hill community where large appliances were taken. This was pretty unusual as most burglars only take stuff they can carry and dispose of quickly. I decided to check any place something like this could be sold to. We had a couple of second hand appliance stores in the area and I felt this was a good place to start. I walked into one on Eastern Avenue and began to casually look around. I didn't have serial numbers so identifying any particular machine was a real long shot. Realizing that I was not there to shop the owner came over and asked what I wanted. I asked if he had bought any washing machines or dryers from a couple of young guys (their description escapes me after all of these years). He became immediately hostile (translation in my mind - guilty). He told me I had no right coming into his store and snooping around, and if I didn't have a warrant I better get the heck out. I made an attempt to reason with him but he was adamant. I reluctantly left vowing to myself that this guy had not heard the last of me. As a patrol officer I did not have the time necessary to devote to a lengthy investigation so I passed my suspicions on to my friends, the Detectives.

I kept my eye on the store and bided my time. Several months later my opportunity presented itself as I knew it would. It was a Friday evening when I saw the guy driving his pickup truck, loaded to capacity, heading toward his shop.

When he stopped at a traffic light I noticed he had no brake lights. I pulled him over and in my best professional demeanor politely asked him for his license and  registration. He recognized me and began to use his attitude with me again. This time, however he was on my turf so I just let him dig himself in deeper. After checking to make sure he was not wanted for anything and the truck was not stolen I wrote him tickets for operating an unsafe vehicle and having an unsecured load on his truck. I also wrote a repair order for him to get his brake lights fixed. He went nuts when I asked him to sign the tickets. I informed him that failing to sign would result in his arrest (a bluff). He signed the tickets and started to get back into his truck. *"Where do you think you're going?"* I asked. *"I'm taking this stuff to my shop if you don't mind"* he replied sarcastically. *"You can go wherever you like, but the truck stays"* I said. *"What the heck are you talking about, you can't keep my truck!"* he countered. *"You see, that's where you're wrong"* I replied. *"This is an unsafe motor vehicle and I'm going to tow it to the impound lot. Of course we can't have all of these valuable appliances sitting out there unprotected so I'm going to submit them to Evidence Control for safe keeping. You will be able to get your truck back on Monday. You'll have to pay the towing charge of seventy-five dollars and three days storage. Once you do that you can stop by and pick up your appliances as long as you can prove ownership and none of them are stolen."* I got the exact reaction I had hoped for; he took a swing at me. I knocked him on his can and handcuffed him. As I was closing the door on the wagon I said, *"I hope this teaches you a lesson. When the nice Policeman comes around and asks you a question, be polite and help him out."*

As a result of taking the load he was carrying on his truck we were able to recover two stolen washers. This gave us probable cause to get a search warrant for his shop which resulted in recovery of four more. He ended up being sentenced to three years for receiving stolen goods. So, I hope you too have learned a lesson from this little story. Always do what the nice Policeman asks.

THE TOUGH GUY & THE STRIPPER

One thing that was not lacking in the Highlandtown/ Canton area was drinking establishments. There was a bar of some sort on almost every corner or so it seemed. They ranged from small neighborhood bars to strip joints. It is not possible to have this much alcohol and not have fights. I have already related several stories about bar fights. This is not as much about the fight as the aftermath. I responded to a call for a fight in the bar at Fleet and Dean Streets. This was a fairly good size bar which featured "Go-Go" girls and pool tables. I arrived and upon entering the bar I saw a guy about six feet four inches, weighing two hundred fifty pounds and holding a broken bottle. No one was making any attempt to  take it away from him and as far as I could see he hadn't used it yet. I heard someone trying to talk him into putting the bottle down so I approached him and asked what was going on. The guy told me that his friend had too much to drink and had gotten a little crazy. He assured me that no one had been hurt and asked if I could give the guy a break because his brother was a cop in another district. I asked for this guy's name and the name of his brother. I then walked over to Sal (the guy with the bottle) and as if nothing was happening I said, *"Hey Sal, how you doin'? Gabe asked me to look after you so I stopped by to see if you needed any help. It looks like you got these guys under control so why don't we get out of here?"*

He dropped the bottle, shook my hand, put his arm around my shoulders and we walked out together.

I stood outside talking to him for a while and then I went back in to insure that everyone was okay. The manager came over and said he didn't want to press charges. Sal had not actually attacked anybody, so he was happy to just let the whole thing drop. I was standing with my back to a pool table (cops always like to have their back covered) when one of the Go-Go girls came over. She walked up and pushed me backward causing me to fall onto the pool table. She then climbed up on top of me and started to push my face between her breasts as she said, *"This is what I like, a real man!"* I was taken completely by surprise. Everyone in the bar started laughing and whistling at us. I know I turned three shades of red. The more I squirmed to get out from under her the worse it got. She started to move up and down on me as if we were having sex. Now I was really embarrassed. I was finally able to get her off of me without resorting to using my night stick (I already learned my lesson on that score). I ran out of the bar like my tail was on fire, to the cheers and whistles of the crowd. It was a long time before I had the nerve to go back in that bar without a back up!

BAD HABIT

Are you a smoker? If you are maybe you can explain the actions of the guy in this story to me. This happened about thirty years ago and I still can't figure him out.

I was traveling southbound on Clinton Street toward the waterfront behind a new red pickup truck. It was about one a.m. on a cold, clear night in the dead of winter. There is never any  traffic this far south on Clinton Street late at night because there wasn't anything there except piers. The road dead ended into the harbor so there is no place else to go (it was a dead end at the time – although they have extended the road now). As we are nearing the end of the road I slow down to turn around, but I notice the truck continues on at a constant speed. I stop my car about fifty yards from the end of the road and watch in amazement as this guy drives his truck right through the barrier and over the sea wall! Fortunately, the rear wheels caught on the guard rail that he had broken through, keeping the truck from plunging into the water.

I rush up to see if the driver is okay and find that the truck is in the water almost to the windshield. The driver climbs out of the window, and I watch as he climbs along the bed of the truck to safety without so much as his shoes getting wet.

I am convinced the guy is drunk. How could anyone not notice the barrier with a flashing yellow light and a big sign saying "Dead End"? After I make sure he is not injured I run him through a field sobriety test. To my amazement he passes. He has no explanation for not seeing the end of the road; he said it was just suddenly there.

I call for a wrecker to pull his truck back onto the road and get it to a garage and we stand there talking while we wait. After five or ten minutes the guy asks me for a cigarette. When I tell him I don't smoke, he turns and starts walking toward his truck. "Where are you going?" I ask. "I'm dying for a cigarette" he replies. Before I can stop him he climbs back down the bed of the truck and leans into the window to get his cigarettes. With that the truck starts to slip over the edge! All I can do is look on as it goes over and begins to sink with him still in the back. The water is freezing cold and I know he can't last long without dying from exposure. I get as close to the edge as I dare and he reaches up and takes my hand. I am able to pull him from the freezing water just as the truck sinks out of sight. I get him back to my car and place him in the back, then get the blanket out of the trunk. As I am handing it to him he holds out his pack of cigarettes and between chattering teeth asks if I have a match!

A REAL PAIN IN THE NECK

It was one of those warm, balmy nights that lull you into a false sense of well-being. I was doing routine patrol near Fells Point at around two thirty a.m. when I observed a car going westbound on Fleet Street. My attention was drawn to the vehicle because it was going slower than the speed limit and weaving across the center line. Normally, this is a sure sign of a driver under the influence of alcohol or drugs. Shortly after getting behind the car I found that this driver was under the influence of something entirely different. I observed a head pop up (from its place in the driver's lap) and look around at me. The erratic behavior of the drive suddenly stopped. Now, not knowing exactly which laws were being broken here I activated my blue lights to pull the vehicle over. Rather than pull to the curb as required the car continued at the same speed. I followed it as it turned south on Broadway and continued for another block. It pulled to the curb and a female passenger got out and ran into the front door of one of the buildings. I approached the car and found that the driver was also a female. Her skirt was pulled up and her clothes were in disarray. The first words out of her mouth were antagonistic. As she continued her belligerent tirade it became apparent that she was not intoxicated. I decided to check her name through the computer to be sure that she was not wanted and then let her be on her way. I took her driver's license back to my car and began to radio the information (no fancy computers in the cars for us in those days). I watched as the driver exited her vehicle and approached my car.

I had just finished relaying the information to the dispatcher when she walked up and demanded her license back. I informed her that the check would take a couple of minutes and asked her to return to her vehicle. With that she reached down and grabbed a handful of my hair. She pulled so violently that my head struck the car door and I saw stars. I knocked her hand away and attempted to exit my vehicle to place her under arrest. She suddenly sat down with her back against my door so I couldn't open it. I slid across the seat and got out of the passenger door. As I came around the back of the car she got up and ran around the front and into the building that her girlfriend had gone into. As she fled up the stairs I caught up with her and, with much difficulty got the handcuffs on her. She began the standard mantra of liberals caught in the "fascist system". She had friends in high places and she would have my badge for this. Little did I know.

After taking her to Women's Detention and booking her I felt my neck beginning to stiffen up. As a result of the whiplash I had suffered I would be unable to turn my head for several days. I did not hear a thing about the case for several months. I decided to inquire as to its status.

I found the female Assistant District Attorney who had been assigned the case and asked her when it was set for trial. The response was very icy and dripping with loathing. She informed me that the charges had been dropped. She stated that I was fortunate to still have my job after what I had done to the "poor girl". When I asked her to elaborate she refused. She said if I didn't want to be the focus of a long investigation by the Internal Investigation Division I would just let it go. I was livid. However, at that stage of my career I was not prepared to fight it. I found out a couple of years later that the passenger that had fled was in fact that very ASA who had dropped the charges!

Unfortunately, that was not the only time a woman bested me in my career. The first time I could claim that it was unexpected (even though I should have been expecting anything). The second time there is no excuse (except the general mindset men have about fighting women).

I received a call to a little corner bar in the 2900 block of O'Donnell Street one cold December night. I wasn't sure what the nature of the problem was; the call was simply "Investigate the Trouble". That was sort of a catch-all when there wasn't a specific incident code to cover it. I was pretty sure it wasn't another bar fight so I ran the other options through my mine (as I usually did in an attempt to be prepared). Well, what I found had not been in my mental checklist, nor was I prepared for it.

As I entered the bar I noticed a few of the "regulars" sitting at the bar and, at the far end was a woman with a baby in front of her on the bar. The baby was quiet and seemed content. The mother was another story. She appeared to be in her early twenties and average height and build. Her face showed the effects of a hard life for her age. The owner of the bar approached me at the door while I was still evaluating the patrons and whispered:

"See that woman at the end of the bar? She's trying to sell her baby for five hundred dollars!"

Okay, that was definitely illegal, so I approached her and asked:

"What are you doing?"

"I'm just trying to have a couple of drinks if it's any of your business."

"What are you doing with the baby in the bar?"

"I couldn't get a babysitter."

"I got a report that you are trying to sell the baby — you want to tell me about that?"

"I'm sick of this kid; I can't go anywhere or do anything anymore. He would be better off with somebody who wants him and I could use the cash — so what?"

That was enough for me, I knew she would be going to Women's Detention and I would be the babysitter at the station until someone from Social Services came to take him to a foster home. I informed her that I was arresting her and asked her very politely to put her hands behind her back so I could handcuff her.

She came off the bar stool like she was shot out of a cannon. Her first punch landed on my nose and had me seeing stars. She then knocked me backwards and as I recovered my balance she jumped on my back and wrapped her arms around my neck and started to chock me. As she was choking me she was also kicking me in the back and legs (thankfully she wasn't wearing high heels). I was able to throw her off my back and onto the floor where I tried to get a hold on her arms and handcuff her. She would have none of it. The way she was kicking, punching and biting there could have been two of her. Finally, the bar owner and a patron grabbed her legs and I was able to get her handcuffed.

As predicted she went to be booked and I spent several hours waiting for Social Services to come and get the baby. The mother underwent some counseling and was able to get custody back a few months later. Never underestimate the ferocity of a mother lion with Post Partum Stress!

NEWS MEDIA

I don't have the actual statistics but back in the 1970's when I joined the Police Department the vast majority of Americans trusted their news sources. In Baltimore we had the big three networks (ABC, CBS, NBC) and two major newspapers The Sun and The News American. As with many things during that time I was as naive as most Americans about the motives and agenda of the American press. It wasn't until years later that I learned that Nazi Germany sent their propaganda minister to the US before World War II to learn how to mislead and mold the people.

Before I get into telling my first eye opening story on the news media I must relate a joke I recently heard that really sums it up.

A little girl was visiting the zoo with her family and while playing got too close to the lion's cage. The lion reached through the bars and grabbed the little girl pinning her against the bars. As the lion was about to tear the girl to pieces a man ran over, struck the lion on the nose with his fist which startled it enough for the man to free the girl and pull her to safety.

It just so happened that a news reporter witnessed the incident and rushed over to the man, "Wow! That was the bravest thing I've ever seen! You saved that little girl's life! I'm going to make sure this is on the front page of the newspaper tomorrow. Tell me, how were you able to react so quickly?"

Well, I'm an off-duty police officer and I was walking home from worship service when I saw the lion grab the girl. I knew I had to act quickly so I ran as fast as I could while saying a little prayer that I would be on time. Thank GOD I was".

The next day the man gets the newspaper and sees the headline: "OFF-DUTY COP ATTACKES AFRICAN AND STEALS HIS LUNCH!"

My story starts one balmy Saturday afternoon in Southeast Baltimore. I was assigned a call for a man selling drugs in the "low rise" projects at Bank and Caroline Streets. Another unit was assigned to back me up as the suspect was reported to be armed with a sawed off shotgun. As I approached from the east my backup came from the west. We both saw the suspect standing on the corner brazenly holding the shotgun in his right hand. As we stopped and exited our cars the suspect ran northeast through the courts. It is truly amazing what the human mind can do, as I was running through the courts chasing this armed subject I remember hearing the children laughing and playing and wondering how they would ever have a chance in life being raised in a place like this. Suddenly as he was rounding a corner and we were gaining on him the suspect turned and fired his shotgun at us. There was no cover and with all of the children around we could not return fire. We continued pursuit and were met by the second round from the double barrel shotgun hastily fired in our direction.

Out of ammo and out of breath the suspect put up little further resistance and was taken into custody. As we walked him back to our cars we saw a crowd had gathered near where the last shot had been fired. There, lying on the ground and bleeding was a girl of 5 or 6 year old. I called for an ambulance and walked my suspect back to the car while my backup performed first aid and comforted the girl. The news media showed up before the ambo and got some footage of the officer with the little girl.

As soon as I got back to the station with the suspect I called my wife to let her know I was okay and briefly told her the facts. I knew she would see it on the news and I didn't want her to worry.

So, how did the news media portray the two officers risking their lives to protect the community? They showed the footage of the officer with the injured child and speculated that it was the officer that had shot her! They interviewed several "residents" (that had not even witnessed the incident) who were happy to tell the story of two wild cops shooting up the projects.

My loving wife, having a very low tolerance for injustice called the news desk and demanded to speak with the reporter. She told him he had his facts all wrong and tried to set him straight. He finally admitted to her that he did not care about what really happened, this was good for their ratings.

The end result of this news fantasy was a lengthy investigation, death threats against the back-up officer that resulted in his being transferred for his own protection. It also made a difficult area even more difficult to police. It helped to further erode the trust between the citizens and the community. This, along with so many stories like it greatly contributed to the police being seen as an occupying army rather than public servants.

THE RAILROAD TUNNEL CAPER

On Halloween night in 1983 I was working the midnight shift in the Southern District. One of my officers got a call at the Ostend Street Bridge to investigate strange lights. I arrived about the same time he did and we were met by a man who told us that there were strange lights and noises coming from the railroad tunnel. We walked about one hundred yards from the road down the tracks to the entrance to the tunnel. We could indeed see flickering yellow and white lights and hear a strange moaning/humming type of sound. The tunnel curved away to our right  so we could only see a short distance from the entrance. Bolstering all of our courage for our entry into the unknown we began walking into the tunnel. I got on the radio and asked the dispatcher to contact the railroad and determine if a train was due anytime soon. I didn't want to be in the tunnel if an express train came through at seventy mph. This was an old railroad tunnel built sometime in the 1850's. It was damp and smelled of mold, smoke and diesel fuel. Looking at the old stone walls I could almost picture the steam trains that first travelled through here with goods and passengers bound for the city or the port to be shipped around the world. As we walked further into the tunnel the lights got brighter and we began to see shadows dancing on the walls and ceiling. The moaning too grew louder.

Finally we reached a point where we could see what was going on. We could see it but neither of us believed what we saw! There was a large bonfire built alongside the tracks with about a dozen people chanting and humming. Some wore black robes, several women were naked dancing around the fire, and there were at least two couples having sex.

There was something hanging from the ceiling over the fire. It was hard to make out in the dancing firelight. As we got closer, still unobserved, I could see that it was a dog which had had its throat cut. Suddenly, one in the group saw us and let out a yell. They all turned and silently began to walk toward us. I was sure I was in one of those zombie movies and if I started shooting these people they would just keep coming. All of them had a sort of blank stare which under the circumstances was rather menacing. I wasn't sure if I should pull my gun (the guy who had killed the dog was still holding a large ceremonial looking knife) or turn and run. I could tell my officer was having the same thoughts as he took a step backwards and almost fell over the tracks. In an effort to take charge I shouted, "What in the world are you people doing here?"

This seemed to break the spell. Suddenly the women were searching for their clothes and the robed figures took off their hoods. A tall thin woman stepped forward and told me that they were devil worshipers who had come here for a Halloween "service".

We marched them out of the tunnel (fresh air was such a relief) and had them transported to the station.

While they were being booked everyone that was in the station stopped by to gawk at them; even for cops who "had seen it all" this was something new. All of them were charged with trespassing on railroad property and the guy with the knife was charged with cruelty to animals for the murder of the dog. The whole incident (including interviews with some of the participants) was on the front page of the newspaper the next day. Thankfully I was not mentioned by name.

WHAT'S SHAKIN' AT CAMDEN YARDS?

Memorial Stadium was the home of the Orioles from 1954 until the Camden Yards stadium was completed in 1992. As a kid I would walk the two miles to the stadium and attended as many baseball games as I could sneak off to.

Everyone knows that police are under paid. No one knows this more than the cops themselves. As a result, most cops work as much overtime as they can. One overtime detail  that I always enjoyed was baseball. Almost from the time I joined the department I put in to work as many games as I could get. It provided a combination of an enjoyable atmosphere and easy money. Except of course if you worked the upper deck Section thirty-four. This section was populated by "Wild Bill" Haggey and the biggest group of beer drinking rowdy baseball fans you've ever laid eyes on. Arrests from Section thirty-four were routine. I never worked that section that I didn't go home soaked in beer (outside only). It was a blue collar baseball park in a blue collar town and the fans loved it.

As Memorial Stadium began to show its age a replacement was planned. When the details about Oriole Park at Camden Yards began to come out everyone was excited.

You could tell from the architectural models that it was going to be a beautiful stadium. We watched with anticipation as construction progressed. It was obvious that this was going to be a terrific baseball park. What was not obvious was the complete change in character. It went from blue collar to "yuppie". From reasonable prices to take the family to a  game it went to, "for our vacation this year let's go to an Oriole game". It was sad to see the change from the point of view of a paying customer; however it was great from the perspective of being paid to be there. The fighting, beer soaked days were gone for the most part. The fans were of a more gentile nature. The Club level where I was assigned most of the time was up scale and classy. Well, maybe not always classy.

I was working overtime in the Club level at an Orioles game one rainy August evening in 1995. The fans were becoming restless due to the long rain delay. Suddenly, coming from the bar I heard women screaming and men yelling and whistling. As I turned and started that way I saw a girl backing out of the bar with her blouse pulled up shaking her breasts around and smiling. She glanced in my direction, and upon seeing me pulled her top down and jumped on the elevator.

Well, I couldn't let her get away with that! I jumped on the next elevator and pursued her. When I got to the first level I saw her going out of the exit doors. I pursued her outside and found her in a crowd waiting under the awning staying out of the rain. As I  approached her she pretended to ignore me but I heard her whisper to her girlfriend, "Oh s---! Here he comes!" I walked over and stood next to her for a moment waiting to see how long she would ignore me. She was good, I finally broke the silence saying, "You realize I'm going to have to confiscate those as evidence?" To that she got a big smile on her face and said, "Okay!" as she pulled her blouse up again revealing her large (and artificially enhanced) breasts. "Please, put those things away, don't you have any shame?" I gasped. "Hey sweetie, I do this for a living at Gayle's Show Bar, there is nothing shameful about it" she replied.

Wanting to extricate myself from this situation as quickly as possible, I told her and her girlfriend to save the show for Gayle's and get the heck out of there. Once they left a woman in her sixties and her husband came over to me. "Isn't that indecent exposure Officer?" the woman asked. "Oh, no ma'am they weren't real!" I replied and walked back inside.

I was somewhat cavalier and unconcerned about her filing a complaint as I had taken to wearing fake name tags (I. M. Tired; I. M. Handsome; I. Dunno, etc). I even had one made especially for working Preakness.

Since almost everyone there is intoxicated I used one to make them go cross-eyed (Z. Kwazuwzcski). I was having fun wearing "I. Dunno" during a period that I was frustrated by stupid questions. I happened to be in the elevator one day when the Police Commissioner (Ed Woods) got on. He looked at me, recognized the face and glanced at my name tag in order to greet me by name. I saw a puzzled look cross his face; he hesitated and then simply said, "Good Morning Sergeant". Later that day I was in the Northwest District doing a favor for the District Commander there when the Captain stopped me and questioned my name tag:

"What are you doing wearing that thing? That is not your name."

"I Dunno" I replied with a grin.

*"I could bring charges against you for your insubordinate attitude and wearing that
stupid name tag you know that don't you?"*

"I suppose if someone in a position of authority wished to show his appreciation for the favor I was doing for his boss and he wanted to be a horse's ass he could charge me. I don't believe I know anyone that stupid do you Captain?" I replied.

The Captain glared at me for a moment and then turned and walked away without another word.

I had the opportunity to aggravate that Captain again a few months later. I was cleaning out the junk from a storage closet in my office when I found a framed picture of him when he was a Sergeant. I dusted it off and went directly up to his new office.

He had been recently transferred to HQ and most of the folks there had not gotten to know him yet. I marched up, handed him the picture and in a loud voice said, "Hey Cap, I thought it was time you came out of the closet!" His face turned red and his nostrils flared. I made a quick exit before he had the chance to start yelling. It turned out he was a pretty decent guy though. After this we developed a mutual respect for each other and have been friends ever since.

Anyway, back to stripper stories. I have to relate this story while we are on the subject. Although I was not directly involved I knew those who were pretty well and it is a story worth telling. I have left out the company name and last names to protect the innocent (if there are any).

It all started when Gary decided to accompany Dave on a customer demo in a large city in the northeast. First, a little background on these two. Gary was a vice president in the company, and although he was a great guy "up tight" is too mild a description. He was the only guy I ever knew who had his blue jeans laundered and starched. On the other hand Dave was an ex-cop from California; very laidback and gregarious. Gary was a happily married man while Dave was a bachelor.

There was a demo scheduled that had the potential to be the largest customer the company ever had. To ensure that everything ran smoothly they brought along four crates of computers pre-loaded with the software they were showing off.

When they arrived at their destination they discovered that their equipment had not made the change in planes and was now being re-routed. They were informed that it would arrive in about three hours. This was an inconvenience but the demo was not until the next day so it posed no serious problems.

Dave – Hey Gary, there is no sense hanging around the airport, I know of a club nearby where we can relax and have a couple of cocktails while we wait.

Gary – I know you Dave, you have a membership in every men's club in America. How sleazy is this one?

Dave – No, this is a nice place. I go there every time I'm in town.

Gary – Okay, but if it's a dive I'm leaving.

So, they grabbed a cab and headed over to the Gentlemen's Club. It was not as bad as Gary had feared but not as nice as Dave had described either.

They stayed for a couple of hours and Gary had two drinks that he nursed while he watched Dave have several. This club, as most clubs of its type had scantily clad, well endowed young ladies serving the drinks. Dave took a liking to one in particular (named Debbie) and the more he drank the larger his tips were. By the time they left the club Dave was completely out of cash.

Their equipment came; they went to their hotel and spent an uneventful night. The next day the demo went well and Gary headed to the airport to catch his flight home. Dave was not scheduled to leave until the following day as he had some follow up meetings to attend to. As Gary was leaving he cautioned Dave about returning to the club.

Gary – Look Dave, stay away from the clubs and just finish up your meetings and work on your paperwork to present to the board next week.

Dave – Yeah, sure Gary. I don't have any intention to return there. I'll see you back at the office on Monday.

That night as Gary lay in bed with his wife Dawn a plan hatched in his fertile mind. He discussed it with his wife and she agreed to help. Gary took the phone and dialed Dave's number then handed it to his wife.

Dave – Hello

Dawn – Hi, is this Dave? This is Debbie from the club.

Dave – Debbie! I'm so glad you called! I waited around the club all day and then found out you were off. I kept bugging that manager of yours but he wouldn't give me your number. I'm glad he at least passed mine on to you.

Gary took the phone from his wife and said,

Gary – Dave, didn't we agree that you wouldn't go back to the club?

Dave – Gary? What the heck are you doing with Debbie? I thought you were going home?

With that both Gary and Dawn began laughing hysterically. As long as I knew these guys this was always a source of embarrassment for poor Dave. It did not, however stop him from frequenting his clubs.

HOORAY FOR HOLLYWOOD

I had the pleasure of meeting several "stars" while working a number of Hollywood films over the years (Sleepless In Seattle; Diner; Tin Men; He Said, She Said; Her Alibi; Homicide; Meteor Man; Runaway Bride and Washington Square). In most cases the duties consisted of long boring hours spent watching equipment (like a trailer full of automatic weapons for Meteor Man) and guarding the star's trailers. It was a tricky balance to be close enough to keep the riff raff out but not witness any questionable behavior on the part of the rightful occupants. Interspersed with the boredom however were some interesting moments. These next three tales relate my experiences when "Tinsel Town" came to Baltimore.

SLEEPLESS IN SEATTLE

Besides baseball another interesting overtime gig was working security for movie shoots. In July of 1993 I worked overtime security on the movie *Sleepless in Seattle* which starred  Meg Ryan. I found Ms. Ryan to be a genuinely nice person. I was assigned as her bodyguard the first time I worked on the film. Almost immediately she made me feel at ease. She was a "regular person". I remember a woman walking by with her ten year old son. She stopped and told Meg that her son was a big fan. Meg asked the young lad if that was true. He said that it was and that he had seen all of her movies. Meg replied, "And you still like me?"

I spent most of that sixteen hour shift talking to actors and crew while Meg did her stuff on camera. I did have the pleasure of eating dinner and breakfast with her and spending several hours in her company.

Later in the month I worked the film again. This time all of the shooting was going on inside, so three officers and I provided security outside. They were shooting on Mulberry Street alongside the Cathedral. A few doors west of the movie shoot is an International Youth Hostel.

Toward early evening I noticed several people on the stoop (Baltimore word for front steps) drinking beer. As the evening progressed one couple began to stand out as they were obviously becoming intoxicated. I was tending to my duties when I heard a great deal of shouting and went to investigate. As I pushed through the crowd that had gathered I saw an attractive young blonde girl (half of the aforementioned couple) taking her tee shirt off and trading with one of the truckers for his. The shouting and whistling resulted from this well endowed  young ladies' lack of underclothing. As she put the trucker's tee shirt on she noticed me and rushed over. Wrapping her arms around me she gave me a big kiss and then pleaded for me to take her away from all of these rowdy men.

I knew that no one outside this circle of the movie crew could have seen this display of public nudity and since they were not complaining I decided not to arrest the intoxicated foreigner (an English citizen as it turned out). When I pried myself loose from her she began to tell me about her travels. She was out to see the world. She had just come from Italy where she had tended bar for a time. I finally convinced her to return to the hostel and allow me to get back to work. That of course was not the end of her. An hour or so later she walked up to me and asked if I had a match. I told her I didn't smoke but she could use the cigarette lighter in my police car. I opened the door and she jumped in to light her cigarette. I couldn't get her back out.

She began to beg me to take her for a ride.

Then, she reached over, grabbed my thigh and said, "I'll do *anything* if you let me drive your Police car!" My response of course was an emphatic *no*.

I told her she was drunk and regardless it was not worth the trouble I would get in if I let her drive (I had no desire to be divorced and unemployed). Her response was, "How do you know it isn't worth the trouble, I'll guarantee you, I am worth it!" Well, this argument went on for several minutes until I finally convinced her that I was not going to let her drive. She kissed me again and said, "Sorry love, it would have been terrific."

She walked back into the hostel and I assumed I had seen the last of her. Wrong again. A short time later I noticed a crowd gathering again so I went to investigate. Looking down the alley I noticed two people under the only street light in the block. It took me a minute to believe I was really seeing what I was seeing. My new friend was completely naked and being "taken" by the guy she had been drinking with. Both had to be aware of the crowd which had gathered (and was cheering them on) but didn't seem to care. The producer came over to me and asked if I could just pretend I hadn't seen it. Her crew had been working since early that morning and this display was bringing them back to life. Once again there were no other witnesses so I agreed. I just walked away shaking my head. Cops sure do lead strange lives!

DINER

Diner was a 1983 Barry Levinson film starring Steve Guttenberg; Daniel Stern; Mickey Rourke and Kevin Bacon. Mr. Levinson's movies were a recounting of his youth growing up in

Baltimore. In this case Diner tells the story of a circle of friends (now in their early twenties) who reunite in 1959 for the wedding of one of their group. The title refers to the Hilltop Diner that was located at Reisterstown Road and Rogers Avenue, their late-night hangout. However, the Hilltop had been converted into a liquor store, so they decided to shoot it in Canton.

The production company bought a diner in New Jersey and had it transported to Baltimore (after the movie it was relocated and functioned as an actual diner for years). They set it up on a vacant lot on Boston Street and named it the Fells Point Diner. They completely transformed everything in the line of

sight from the diner. Although they were shooting in June the movie took place in December 1959 so they had all of the homes in the area strung with Christmas lights. People driving through the neighborhood that did not know a movie was being shot thought the whole neighborhood had gone nuts.

The parking lot of the diner as well as the lot across the street was staged with vintage 1950's cars to complete the scene.

I was prepared for a quiet, boring night as all of the scenes were being shot inside the diner and I was keeping an eye on the equipment outside. The Director had provided me with one of their walkie-talkies in case they needed me for something. At around two a.m. I heard a frantic voice come over the radio, "Officer! Officer! We need you inside the diner right away!" I was just across the street so I was inside in under a minute. The Director ran over and told me they were shooting the scene when a guy wandered in and started acting crazy. When they asked him to leave he threatened violence. I could see the guy surrounded by several of the film crew and as I approached I recognized him right away. We had attended high school together ten years prior and had always gotten along well. "Hey Pete!" I yelled. "What's going on?" I could see that Pete (Petro Screcuzk was his given name) was high on something. It took him a minute to recognize me in my uniform, but once he did a big grin crossed his face. "Hey man, good to see you. All I want is a hamburger. I came into this stinkin' diner and asked for a hamburger and they tried to throw me out!" I knew trying to reason with him in this state of inebriation would be fruitless so I tried another tactic. "Pete, the food here really stinks, and the service is worse. Let's walk down the block to the Sip & Bite and I'll buy you a burger, okay?" This seemed to mollify him and we turned and walked out of the diner together. As we walked down the block Pete said he was pretty tired and decided to go home instead of getting something to eat. Just before he left he asked me if I had the homework for the next day – he had not had the time to do it. He was very concerned about getting into trouble with Mr. Jackson who was always picking on him because he was Ukrainian. I told him I had it and would let him have it in the morning so he went home happy.

I went back and told the Director that Pete would not cause him any more trouble. You would have thought I just solved the crime of the century. He was so grateful that they could get back to shooting (time is money)!

METEOR MAN

I think one of the strangest films I worked on was Meteor Man. The Meteor Man is a 1993 superhero comedy written by, directed by, and starring Robert Townsend with supporting roles by Bill Cosby and some other notable actors.

It was during this time that Bill Cosby was doing those Jell-O Pudding Pop ads on TV. As a result, every time he came out of his trailer he was inundated with neighborhood kids yelling to him for some Pudding Pops. He got so tired of this that at one point he yelled back, "You want Pudding Pops get a job, earn some money and go buy them!"

In the movie the bad guys were trying to kill the superhero (I don't remember why) so there were several scenes where they tried "drive by" shootings. It was pretty cool how they did this. The special effects guys would stick "squibs" (small fire crackers) on the walls, cars, trees and everything in the line of fire.

The bad guys would drive by and shoot blanks from the car and the exploding squibs made it appear that the bullets were striking all around the hero. I could not believe the cache of weapons they had for this film. One entire wall of the equipment trailer was lined with automatic weapons.

As we were shooting in West Baltimore (a notorious drug haven) we had a officer in that trailer at all times.

There was one scene where the superhero was just learning to fly and was peeking into a second floor window. This was accomplished via a harness and cables of course. However, every time they got halfway through the scene the  Director would yell, "CUT" and send one of his gophers off to the house next door. After the third time he called for me on the radio. When I got there he explained that the woman in the house there kept opening her shades and sticking her face up to the window. After politely asking her three times to stop he had had enough. He wanted me to go in there and arrest her. I had to inform him that movie or no movie the woman had a right to look out her window. He was perplexed; what did I mean – the Director was "all powerful" on the set and not to be disobeyed! One of his assistants (with a bit more common sense) suggested that they offer the woman money to stay inside. The Director thought that was a wonderful idea and sent the guy over with fifty dollars for the woman. That did the trick (for now) and the scene got finished. It did not take long for word to get around though. In almost every scene after that they had to pay someone to stay out of the shot!

Other than keeping the women from molesting Tom Selleck and seeing just how self absorbed some of the stars could be those were the highlights of my brushes with fame.

NIGHTMARES

We all have stories about the funny little things we do to other cops we find unawares (asleep). I have already gone into great detail on one of them. Now I would like to share a couple more with you.

There is an isolated wooded area in the Carroll Park Golf Course where one particular officer liked to spend his nights. He had been told time and again that it was not a good idea to be "unaware" in such an isolated area but he failed to heed my warnings. I decided it was time to teach him a lesson. One dark windy night I waited to be sure he was very relaxed and comfy. I used all of my ninja techniques to get to an area just out of sight around a curve. I elicited the cooperation of the wagon man and with the aid of the winch we pulled a fallen tree across the road. This was winter time so it gets light just prior to shift change. True to form the officer started to head for the station at seven thirty a.m. When he came around the bend he found the tree down and no way around it. As it was too large for him to move he was thoroughly stuck. He called for me to meet him and I told him I was not available, requesting that he meet me in the station. I was determined to force him to admit on the radio that he was stuck.

Finally, after exhausting all possible excuses he stated that the wind had blown a tree down in his path and he was unable to get the car out. That brought forth all sorts of comments and noises over the radio. Half the shift went to gawk at this poor officer's predicament. Of course it was obvious to anyone who looked that the tree had been dragged and not blown over.

It took until ten a.m. for the forestry service to arrive and remove the tree so he could go home (I wouldn't let the other officers pitch in and move it for fear of sustaining injuries not in the line of duty). The next night when he came in he gave me an overtime slip for two and a half hours. I suggested that he attach a complete report to justify the overtime, including his reason for being in such an isolated area. I also suggested that he explain how a tree that had obviously been long dead had "fallen" and rolled that far from its original position. I could see the wheels turning as these facts fell into place. He tore the overtime slip up and threw it in the trash. As he walked out of the office he assured me that he understood how dangerous it can be back there in the woods and would not return unless he got a call there. For months afterwards and even to this day the word "Timber!" brings laughter to all who were there.

Other times it is just a matter of the opportunity presenting itself. A raccoon had been hit by a car and had expired on the side of the road.

Upon finding an officer sound asleep behind the school I put the two together and came up with a plan.

I got a couple of other guys together and we took the raccoon and quietly placed it with arms and legs spread open on the officer's windshield. We then stuck a firecracker in its ear and lit it. Standing back we watched as the firecracker went off startling the officer awake. Seeing the grotesque figure staring in at him had the desired effect. He bailed out of the car pulling his revolver to defend himself from the smoking monster which was attacking him. The roar of laughter brought him back to reality as he meekly put his gun away, removed the raccoon and drove away without a word.

ARIZONA SHOOTING

In the hierarchy of the police department a Deputy Commissioner is akin to one of the gods on Mount Olympus compared to a lowly Sergeant. The little I knew of DC Michael Zotos did not ease my apprehension when I was told I had been chosen to accompany him to Phoenix, Arizona for a conference. In an effort to impress the DC with my spirit of cooperation and fiscal responsibility I went to his office to see if he wished to share a cab to the airport from HQ. The DC was not impressed. Apparently he thought I was being a smart aleck (me?). A Deputy Police Commissioner does not ride in a cab. His driver would take him to the airport in his departmental car; I could take the cab (or better yet a bus) by myself.

The big day finally arrived and I, being an inexperienced traveler arrived at the airport very early. I did not check any of my luggage because I did not trust the airline with it. They had already called our flight to board when the DC finally showed up. I had been worrying that he would miss the flight. When he arrived he went and sat by himself while the other passengers were boarding. I walked over with my luggage and made an attempt at being pleasant. The DC barely looked at me. He said, *"Go ahead and board, I'll be along when the crowd thins out."* Okay, he already thought I was a smart aleck, so since he was acting like a jackass I thought I'd play my part. I set one of my bags down next to him and said, *"Since you checked all of your bags how about carrying this one on for me?"* At that I turned and walked away.

Once I was in my seat I watched to see the DC board, hoping he would not leave my bag behind. Thankfully, when he entered the plane he was carrying my bag while giving me a look that would turn a lesser man to stone. Whether it was planned or by chance we did not have adjoining seats. The first leg of the journey was fairly short as we had to change planes in Nashville, Tennessee. There was a short layover between flights so we went to refresh ourselves. The DC said he was going to get some fruit to snack on and went off in search of a suitable vendor. When he returned to the gate just before boarding he had an apple in his hand and a banana sticking out of his pocket. I could not resist the temptation, DC or not. As he approached I said, *"Hey Boss, is that a banana in your pocket or are you glad to see me?"* His face turned red, I could see a dozen retorts pass through his mind. Finally, in a low menacing voice he replied, *"They warned me about you, you son of a B&*%$# but I didn't believe them"*.

Once again our seats were located in separate rows so I made conversation with my seatmates for the long flight. The rest of that day and most of the next were uneventful.

Our Motorola rep (Eric) had arranged for entertainment after the conference concluded for the day. He asked that we change into comfortable clothes and meet him in front of the hotel. We were not sure what to expect but what we found had never even crossed our minds. When we walked out of the hotel, there stood Eric next to an open Jeep with a true to life cowboy behind the wheel.

He informed us that he had arranged a Jeep tour of the desert followed by drinks at sunset and an outdoor grilled steak dinner. It sounded great! I climbed in the back with Eric and the DC got in front with our guide Wally. Before he started the Jeep Wally told everyone to buckle up. Both Eric and I had simple lap belts in the back that went on without a problem. The DC however had a lap/shoulder belt combination and it was not cooperating. Every time he pulled it out it got stuck. It would come to within six inches of closing but never quite make it. With each pull the DC was getting more and more frustrated. It didn't help when Wally began to harass him with comments like, *"Common fat boy git that belt around your gut! What's a matter fat boy you have too many donuts today? Look fat boy, you gotta wear that belt, it's the law around these parts. Hey fat boy, you don't git that belt on I got some rope in the back I'll tie ya to the seat!"* Finally red faced and winded the DC got the seat belt on and we were off on our adventure.

The first hour was very educational. Our guide was very knowledgeable about the plants and geology of the desert. He threw in some interesting local history and kept us enthralled. At one point we met another Jeep in the back country. Wally pulled up next to it and began talking to the  female driver. After he introduced us and we joked around a bit he told her he would see her at dinner.

Once we were away he informed us that she was his wife. He further enlightened us regarding the riff the marriage had caused between her and her rich parents. Wally was not the man they saw their little girl marrying. He was a desert and hunting guide, rodeo rider (he said he had broken nearly every bone in his body at one time or another) and had been an extra in several movies. He was a general, all around free spirit who had no use for a nine-to-five job.

Suddenly, in the middle of nowhere Wally stopped the Jeep in a dry wash and told us all to get out. He reached under the seat and pulled out two six shooters. These were in addition to the two he was wearing tied down in typical cowboy  fashion. With a grin he said, *"Well boys, I don't rightly know how it's done in the big city, but out here you don't go traipsing off into the desert with a man you don't know who's wearing a side arm. I'll tell you what I'm gonna do. I'm gonna set up some bottles over there and you boys are gonna have to shoot 'em. If you hit a bottle you git a ride back, if you don't you walk!"* With that Wally handed a pistol to the DC. He took careful aim and fired. A miss! He tried to control his breathing, took aim again and, a miss! Now Wally started on him again. With each miss Wally antagonized and belittled the DC. As with most cowboys and their six shooters they only load five rounds. The DC fired his fifth and last round and missed! I guess all of those years of "call in qualifying" (inside joke for BPD) at the range had come back to haunt him. Wally laughed and handed the other gun to Eric saying, *"O.K. son, you got the chance to be a hero. If you can hit two bottles you win a ride back for fat boy here."* Eric, who had never fired a gun before set about doing his best imitation from cop shows he had seen.

He got the grip down but failed when it came to stance and sight picture. With each successive shot he was getting closer to the bottles. It was not until his last shot that he was able to hit one. You could see the relief and pride on his face until the DC  gave him that look that said, "What about me?" While Eric had been shooting Wally reloaded the first gun. He turned to me and said, *"Well, it looks like it's up to you to git fat boy home. How about it?"* I just stood there making no attempt to take the offered pistol. I looked him in the eye and said, *"I'm sorry, I'm afraid of guns. I'd rather not."* Now Wally looked disgusted and the DC's mouth dropped open. We had not told Wally what we did for a living; he assumed that we worked with Eric at Motorola. Wally began to tell me how safe guns are and how if I didn't even try he was going to leave us out there.

I played my frightened role for a few more minutes and then reluctantly took the gun. I really hammed it up for a bit, my hand shaking and my breathing rapid. The DC was looking at me like I was crazy. When I had strung them along as far as I could I turned and in rapid  succession I shot four bottles. I then turned to Wally with the gun pointed at the ground at his feet (and one round left) and said, *"I don't know how it's done out here, but where I come from you don't hand a man a loaded gun unless you know what he intends to do with it!"*

Well, Wally started laughing so hard he almost doubled over. *"You sand bagged me, you sure enough did"* he laughed, *"I guess we all ride now"*.

We drove on for a bit and stopped on the top of a bluff looking out over the desert. Wally took out a cooler with beer and sodas. We sat there and drank a few beers (Wally drank

soda) while we watched the sun set and told stories about other adventures we had undertaken. Once it got dark it was time to head off to dinner. We drove a short distance to what had, until recently been a ghost town. Some enterprising gentlemen had gotten together and opened a restaurant there. It was set up like an old ranch and the cooking was done outside on open fires. We got a table out

under the stars and ordered our steaks. A short time later Wally's wife arrived with another girl and no customers. As they sat down Wally asked where her tour was. She replied, *"Bunch of darn Germans, I left them at McDonalds!"* The other girl turned out to be another tour

driver and a rodeo rider like Wally. In answer to a comment from the DC she answered, *"Mr. I'm the kind of girl your momma warned you about. I'll put a hurtin' on you, believe that"*.

We thoroughly enjoyed the rest of the evening, laughing and telling stories. Wally's wife really got a kick out of our little shooting scrape. On the way back I asked Wally to stop the Jeep if he saw a rattle snake. I wanted to take a rattle or head back as a souvenir. As we were driving down a dirt path in the desert at about thirty mph he suddenly stopped the Jeep.

"You wanted a rattler didn't you?" he asked. *"I just heard one, let's go git him."* We got out of the Jeep and started walking back along the road with the headlights illuminating our way. I was amazed that he could have heard a snake while driving at that speed. Sure enough about twenty feet off the road I saw a big rattler  heading into the brush. Wally went after it but it got into the brush before he could grab it. The disappointment must have shown on my face. Wally said, *"I won't chase a rattler into the bush, not no more. I used to come out here right regular and catch snakes. I'd git me a big sack of 'em and then take 'em home and throw 'em in the freezer. The next mornin' I'd git up, dump 'em in the sink and run 'em under cold water to thaw 'em out. Then I'd skin 'em and sell the meat to the restaurants and the skins and rattles to the tourist shops. Well, one evening I finished up catchin' a bunch of rattlers and started home. I ran into an old pard that I hadn't seen for a while and we decided to have a few drinks. It turned into a few more than a few and I got home real late. I threw the snakes in the freezer and went to bed. It must of only been a couple of hours later when I got up. I went into the kitchen and pulled the bag out of the freezer. When I dumped it into the sink I got the surprise of my life. Those snakes were just cold enough to be real ornery. One of 'em jumped up and latched on to my arm. I was hootin' and a hollerin' and runnin' around that kitchen dodging snakes and tryin to git 'em put back in the bag. I had to gather 'em all up before I could git myself over to the hospital. Well sir that was the end of my snake huntin days!"*

The rest of the conference was dull and uneventful. We did find the DC a nice girlfriend, (pictured) but her dad would never let them spend any time alone. The DC and I, although not becoming fast friends did develop a mutual respect for each other.

My associates all boarded planes and returned to Baltimore, while I remained to enjoy Arizona for a few days before my next conference with the International Association of Chiefs of Police (IACP).

My next Arizona adventure was made possible by the Phoenix Police Department. I had arranged to go on a ride along on the four p.m. to midnight shift. The Officer (John) picked me up at my hotel and we jumped right into the thick of it. Answering calls for service for a prowler, a domestic and a fight in progress we worked up an appetite. John took me to a western style restaurant where the waitresses were dressed as cowgirls, including a pair of six guns. When our waitress came over I could not contain myself. I asked if the guns were real. She gave me one of those looks that says, "not another one" and replied, "You get one step out of line sugar and you'll find out!" There was no question of stiffing her on her tip. We had an enjoyable meal and then headed back to protecting the public.

John asked me if I had seen the television show *Emergency 9-1-1* which had featured the Phoenix PD. I had seen the story and said so. It had shown a woman caught in a flash flood being rescued from the top of her car as the water rose to engulf her. John said that he had been the first officer on the scene and had coordinated the rescue. The only problem had been that he had parked his brand new cruiser too close and the rising water had carried it away! Hero one minute, fool the next.

John took me out to their air unit and introduced me to the pilots. They invited me to come back and fly with them when I had time. I did not need to be asked twice.

The next night I returned to the airport raring to go. The Phoenix PD had just taken delivery of a new fleet of Notar helicopters (Notar stands for No Tail Rotor). They were sleek and quiet and held four occupants. The only problem was that they could not carry a full load and take off if the temperature exceeded one hundred ten degrees (fairly common in Phoenix). With the  doors off and the sun low in the sky we lifted off into the wild blue yonder. My companion in the passenger compartment was an officer from the academy. They require all of their trainees to do a fly-along while in the academy. She was very nervous. The first time I leaned out the door to take a picture she almost screamed. The pilot told her to just take a deep breath and stare at her feet.

The city was beautiful from the air. With Squaw Peak dominating the skyline and the city stretching over four hundred square miles it was very impressive.

We flew low over Squaw Peak and all of the hikers stopped to wave (in stark contrast to those who stand on the roof of the projects and shoot at the helicopter in Baltimore). I flew with them for five hours and we only had one real incident.

A robbery suspect was believed to be hiding in a wooded area so we flew over to illuminate it so ground officers could search. We kept going in a circle for about ten minutes and I was getting pretty dizzy. I was happy to get back to the hanger and get my feet back on the ground.

While I was visiting Phoenix I decided to look up Harry "Moose" Blazer. I had been doing business with him via the mail and telephone and he asked me to stop by while I was out his way. Harry was a cop in the Surprise Arizona Police Department. How I longed to go on a ride-along with him – especially if we could serve a search warrant.

Imagine knocking down a door and rushing in shouting, "SURPRISE POLICE!" He and a friend owned a badge/patch designing company which ended up doing most of the departments in the four corners area. He had built an addition onto his house to display his collection of three thousand police badges! While admiring his display I noticed a couple of badges from Baltimore. Moose noticed and asked me not to take the badge numbers and trace them as he was sure they had been reported "lost". I had an enjoyable visit with Moose and added a couple of new items to my badge collection.

I have always been a fan of Louis L'Amour and his books on the old west. I was discussing this with Harry when he mentioned that there was an old 1880's era steam train that went from Williams to the Grand Canyon. He also mentioned the old silver mining town of Jerome that was an interesting place to visit. It would be a great way to see the canyon and experience the old west. I loved the idea and made arrangement to do just that. The following adventure is written in the style made so popular by my favorite author.

Rising early, as is my habit, I planned to explore some canyons down near Jerome. As the sun began its slow ascent heralded by a symphony of birds I noticed a storm approaching from the west. Deciding I wanted no parts of the flash floods such storms bring, I changed my plans and headed for the train station in Williams.

That something was in the wind any tenderfoot could see. Passengers were lounging about the platform waiting for the train as usual. What caused a knot to grow in my stomach was the salty characters who stayed near their horses watching and waiting. Waiting for what though? I cursed the shortsighted laws that  had forced me to travel without my sidearm. Now, as I watched these outlaws, every one armed, I knew we were in for nothing but trouble.

I heard the train long before I could see it. The old steam locomotive came chugging around the bend and stopped at the station, throwing out a cloud of steam that rolled over everything, passengers, horses, and buildings, obscuring them all from view. I boarded with the other passengers, feeling six pairs of eyes watching me as I did. Being the only unattached man there I knew they would wonder what I was about. As soon as the trouble started they would come for me, of that I was sure.

As the train pulled from the station I looked around the passenger cars. There would be no help here. Oh, there were several men, but they were either too young or too old to stand up to the likes of those outlaws.

I remained alert as the train picked up speed leaving Williams behind. We were only a mile or so from town when I

heard the first shot ring out. Then several more shots accompanied by whooping and hollering. I watched as three riders approached on each side of the train. One at a time they boarded, guns out and ready for trouble. What I would give for a rifle or shotgun. Even as I wished it I knew it would be futile. A shootout now would only hurt innocent people. Let these no accounts take their loot and move on, as long as they didn't hurt any of these good people.

These guys were not amateurs, of that I was sure. I heard one of them running across the roof of the car and then saw him jump to the platform at the rear of the car. On some signal I could not see one man entered from each end of the car. Firing a shot into the ceiling they announced the holdup. Women screamed and children hid behind their mother's petticoats. I knew that if I handed over my wallet with my tin star in it I was in for serious trouble. I had to think of something fast. Taking a small leather pouch I had I made a show of throwing it out the window. When the masked gunman yelled I replied, "I'd rather some trail bum get my money than you hombres." That he was angry I had no doubt.

Just as he came toward me to administer whatever punishment he believed appropriate he noticed the young girl seated across the aisle from me. His attention went immediately to her ample figure. As long as he just looked I was happy for the reprieve. However, as I expected he had decided to take her along as entertainment for him and his friends. This I could not allow. As I stood to intervene a shot rang out. It came from the other end of the car but I neither heard nor felt it strike. The man holding the girl and I turned as one. Having been in this type of situation before I knew at a glance what I must do.

I put my foot behind the outlaw's and pushed him backward while pulling the girl from his grasp. The gun fell from his hand as he reached for the seats to break his fall. Almost before the gun hit the floor I was on top of it. He kicked out with his foot trying to kick it away from me. I blocked the kick with my leg and turned the gun on him. With that, and the Deputy who had just shot his accomplice standing behind me the fight went right out of him. As the Deputy led the hombre away the young girl turned to me, the relief and gratitude showed in her pale blue eyes…

Suddenly the train whistle sounded and I awoke from my daydream. Finally, the train had arrived at its destination - The Grand Canyon.

As I stepped off with the other passengers I was struck by its immense beauty!

I could see why folks would brave this wild country full of outlaws to see it. I cannot even attempt to put my feelings or its beauty into words. It was as if I was small and insignificant and rich beyond measure all at the same time. A peaceful feeling washed over me as I watched a hawk soaring overhead. Now, finally I knew what the Indians meant when they say you must live in beauty with mother Earth.

The time came to return to work and the second half of my assignment. I arrived at the resort hotel where the IACP was putting me up and found the registration desk for the conference where I picked up the agenda for the days to come. I was both excited and nervous. This was the first time I had ever been to something like this and I didn't know a soul there. The first thing that jumped out at me on the front of the schedule was a hospitality suite at the hotel. This would be my chance to meet some of the attendees and have a few free drinks. I located the suite which was right next to the pool. There were quite a few gentlemen (not ladies so much back then) and I saw the IACP guy Chuck who had invited me. We had a few beers and he introduced me around. All in all I was having a pleasant evening. That is until I mentioned to Chuck how grateful I was to the IACP for bringing me to the conference and paying all of my expenses. At first he gave me a strange look which turned into a big grin. He picked up the agenda for the next morning and pointed at it. My name jumped out at me from the list of guest speakers for the following morning. I was listed as an expert in Mobile Data Computing and was scheduled to give a one hour presentation on the subject. "Nothing for nothing" Chuck said. Talk about butterflies!

I went directly to my room and began to prepare as best I could on such short notice.

In the morning I found that they were busing us to the University of Arizona where the conference was being held. All I can say is that I was glad I was the first speaker. If I would have seen how well prepared and dynamic some of the other speakers were I'm not sure I could have followed them. My only saving grace was my sense of humor. I started off by saying, "Wow, I'm not used to facing this many people without a shotgun in my hand! I told a few jokes to loosen them up and then told them of the MDC project my department was in the midst of. Everyone was polite and applauded at the end and I was subsequently invited to repeat my presentation at the international conference in St. Louis so I suppose I did a decent job. But one story at a time here. I was followed by a guy from the Chicago PD who did an outstanding job. We were then given a break for lunch, which they were providing in another building. The conference was being held in a large lecture hall and the lights had been dimmed for the slide presentation so when we exited into the bright Arizona sun it was almost blinding. As I mentioned earlier, we were on the campus of University of Arizona which is a lovely place. It is also quite naturally full of college girls, to the dismay of one of my colleagues. He walked out of the lecture hall into the bright sunshine and as his eyes were still adjusting as a cute coed walked by. The poor guy continued walking forward while craning his neck to watch the girl in the short skirt. Suddenly we heard a big splash! The poor guy had walked right into a large reflecting pool and fallen flat on his face!

Besides the embarrassment this poor guy had to sit the rest of the day in a wet suit as he had no way to get back to the hotel to change.

The next day we were taken to the Phoenix PD's new state-of-the-art headquarters building. It was on this memorable day that I met Bruce Shannon. At the time he was a Major in the US Air Force in their IT section. We hit it off immediately and have been friends ever since. During the evenings after a long day of lectures I made good use of the IACP hospitality suite and met some interesting people from departments all over the country. One night Bruce and I decided to check out some of the local establishments so we asked the bell captain where the action was. He directed us to Bobbie MaGee's Bar and offered to drive us there.

When we entered the place was packed to the rafters. We walked over to the bar and I ordered a beer. That's it; all I said was "Bud". The bar maid says, "You're not from around here are you?" How much of an accent can you distinguish out of the word Bud? She was good! We stood in a corner drinking our beer, listening to the music and watching all of the strange people. At one point Bruce observed two girls walk in the front door. He turns to me and says, *"Whoa! Look at those two would you?"* I glanced at them and turned away. Bruce was persistent and watched them for several minutes. They began to walk toward a vacant table near us and I could see that Bruce was getting excited. He commented on how beautiful they were and asked why I wasn't checking them out.

"I'm not really into transvestites" I replied. You could have knocked Bruce over with a feather. After staring for several minutes he finally conceded that I was right. Then in his dry, brilliant sense of humor he said, *"Well, do you want to buy them a drink or what?"* Of course I did not and that was the end of that, or so I thought. Six months later Bruce brought his wife Laura to Baltimore to meet Barbara and me for dinner. When the waiter asked if we wanted cocktails Bruce turned to me and said, *"I still owe you a drink from Phoenix don't I. Or do you owe me one? No that's right I owe you because you bought that last round for the transvestites!"* You could have heard a pin drop. Both of our wives sat staring at us and the waiter just stood there dumfounded. I am still explaining that one.

BACKFIRED ANNIVERSARY

We had just been assigned a newly promoted Commanding Officer. Being transferred into a new command is a difficult transition; add to that the new promotion and you raise the stress level (on both sides) exponentially. I am always looking for ways to break the ice and make people feel comfortable. In that vein I planned an anniversary surprise for the new CO. I came in an hour early and "decorated" his office.

I had a lookout posted to warn me when he arrived for work. Everyone crowded around the back entrance to his office so we could jump in and yell surprise when he entered the front door. As there was an audio portion to this surprise I had to hit "play" on the cassette player just before he entered. I had just quietly closed the back door when I heard him open the front and the pre-recorded message began. I immediately noticed that the rest of the participants had disappeared. Since everything was happening so quickly I didn't think about why they ran off I just opened the office door and stepped in. There stood the CO with his wife and two young daughters looking at the blowup sex doll seated at his desk and listening to the pre-recorded woman moaning in ecstasy (from the movie *When Harry Met Sally*)! Okay smart aleck what do you do now. I did the only thing I could under the circumstances; I apologized to the ladies for the tasteless joke, turned off the sound effects and walked out dragging the doll behind me. That's when I discovered where my backup went. The lookout had warned them that the boss had his family with him but they chose not to mention that to me. When I came out they were in the hall laughing and enjoying my embarrassment immensely.

After his family left the CO called me into his office and informed me that his wife had thought it was very funny but was going to have a difficult time explaining the purpose of the doll to the kids. He was a pretty good sport and did not hold it against me. The rest of the unit had a good laugh at my expense for weeks to come.

A REAL MAN

It was in the early 1990's when the AIDS epidemic was just beginning. For some reason the department thought that adult police officers still may not know how to put a condom on. The unpleasant duty of demonstrating this to In-Service classes fell on Lt. Joe Darchicourt. Seriously and with a straight face the good Lieutenant demonstrated the correct process by putting a condom over three of his fingers. Keeping a straight face was quite a feat with the comments and laughter from the class. Later that day we had a class that was supposed to help us learn how to speak to a group. I don't remember the instructor's name, but she assigned everyone in the class a word. You were required to give a thirty second talk on it immediately and then return the next day and give a five minute talk on it. Some of the words were really out there. Ron Roof got "Chia Pet". Others were more conventional. By some fluke I got "rubber".

During my initial thirty seconds I spoke about rubber tires, floor mats and other normal stuff. After class that day I went and prepared my talk and my props.

The next day when my turn came around it went something like this: *"Everyone remembers the class we had yesterday with Lt. Darchicourt. Now I hate to disparage him, but after watching him put his rubber on I can tell you he isn't a real man."* At that I took out my first prop, an elephant condom bought at the gag store.

"I'll show you how a real man puts on a rubber" I said as I rolled the condom up my arm to my shoulder! The class went wild, the instructor turned red. "But wait, I'm not finished yet. For you guys on a tight budget I also have the "poor man's rubber". With this I took out a rubber glove on which I had written a day of the week on each finger. *"The beauty of this is, if you're fortunate enough to use up all five before the week is done, you can turn it inside out, rinse it off and start again!"* That was all the instructor could take. She rushed up and ordered me to cease and desist and take my seat. Poor Ron had a rough time following this with his Chia Pet talk.

'...and you didn't forget the condoms, did you?'

SPREADING GOODWILL

In 1998 I was assigned to attend a conference in San Francisco for a week. I decided that it would be interesting to see a little of the country on the way so I decided I would fly into Salt Lake City and take a trip up to Yellowstone (at my own  expense of course). I was telling a friend of mine (John Kowalchcz) about this while we were working overtime at a baseball game one evening. I don't know anyone who likes to travel more than John. After hearing my itinerary he decided to tag along. The arrangements were made to fly to Salt Lake City on Southwest Airlines, rent a car and drive to Jackson Hole, WY. We would spend the first night there and then proceed to the Old Faithful Lodge in Yellowstone National Park. The trip, with two wild and crazy guys like us did not bode well for the general population. Either one of us could make the most stoic, serious mind person in the room roll with laughter. Put us together and it is a recipe for a laughter epidemic.

The fun didn't take long to get started. We had just reached cruising altitude on our flight and the Flight Attendants had started providing refreshments. Now John and I are both above average in size, so when they started passing out bags of peanuts that weren't even big enough to satisfy a Baltimore mouse we knew it called for drastic action.

When the flight attendant came by with the peanuts I told her that our friend "Sam" was in the restroom and we would take his peanuts for him. She looked dubious but went along. Later when she came through with the drinks we again said Sam was in the restroom and took his drink. The flight attendant came back a bit later and handed me a note which said, *"Hey guys, I met a beautiful mermaid in the restroom! We are running away to get married so don't look for us. By the way, go ahead and eat my peanuts for me."* When I read it out loud several of the surrounding passengers (who had heard my previous requests) began to laugh. As we ate we began joking and slinging banter back and forth. Things like:

John: Did you hear that scoundrel Joe Allen died last week? I didn't attend the funeral, but I sent a nice letter saying I approved of it.

Me: I've never killed a man, but I have read many obituaries with great pleasure.

John: Old Joe had no enemies, but he was intensely disliked by his friends.

Me: Yeah, He loved nature in spite of what it did to him.

John: Did you hear what happened at City Hospital yesterday? A man ran into the ER and yelled, "My wife's going to have her baby in the cab!" The ER doctor grabbed his bag, rushed out to the cab, lifted the lady's dress, and began to take off her underwear. That's when he noticed that there were several cabs there, and he was in the wrong one!

Did you hear what happened to JD? He was working on his motorcycle on his patio and his wife was in the house in the kitchen. JD was racing the engine on the motorcycle and somehow, the motorcycle slipped into gear.

JD, still holding the handlebars, was dragged through a glass patio door and the motorcycle dumped onto the floor inside the house. His wife, hearing the crash, ran into the dining room and found JD lying on the floor, cut and bleeding, the motorcycle lying next to him and the patio door shattered.

His wife ran to the phone and summoned an ambulance. Because they lived on a fairly large hill, she went down the several flights of long steps to the street to direct the paramedics to JD. After the ambulance arrived and transported him to the hospital, she up-righted the motorcycle and pushed it outside. Seeing that gas had spilled on the floor, she obtained some papers towels, blotted up the gasoline, and threw the towels in the toilet. JD was treated at the hospital and was released to come home. After arriving home, he looked at the shattered patio door and the damage done to his motorcycle. He became despondent, went into the bathroom, sat on the toilet and smoked a cigarette. After finishing the cigarette, he flipped it between his legs into the toilet bowl while still seated. His wife, who was in the kitchen, heard a loud explosion and JD screaming. She ran into the bathroom and found him lying on the floor. His trousers had been blown away and he was suffering burns on the buttocks, the back of his legs and his groin. She again ran to the phone and called for an ambulance. The same ambulance crew was dispatched and she met them at the street. The paramedics loaded JD on the stretcher and began carrying him to the street. While they were going down the stairs to the street accompanied by his wife, one of the paramedics asked the wife how JD had burned himself. She told them and the paramedics started laughing so hard, one of them tipped the stretcher and dumped JD out. He fell down the remaining steps and broke his arm.

The lady across the aisle from us was laughing so hard she had tears in her eyes. She turned to me and said, "You guys are so funny, did the airline hire you as in-flight entertainment?" I got a very serious look on my face and replied, "Oh, no ma'am it's a condition of our parole. They let us out early as long as we promised to make people laugh where ever we go." The color drained from her face, she turned around and faced front and never looked our way the rest of the flight. As we were about to deplane, just to have a little more fun I asked her if she needed help carrying her bag.

We had to change planes in Kansas City for the second leg of our journey. I almost didn't make it out again.

We had to go to a different terminal to catch our connecting flight. The setup was such that both new arrivals and those changing planes used the same entrance. This meant that everyone had to go through security again. John went through the metal detector without a problem. As I went through something caused it to go off. The security person was a large masculine looking female completely devoid of a sense of humor. Of course, John sensing this made a comment like, *"You better check him real good, he's a dangerous man."* Our security person, taking John at his word had me stand with my legs spread and my arms extended. In an example of perfect timing, the lady from across the aisle walked up just in time to see this. She hurried through the other checkpoint and continued looking back at me until she went around a corner and out of sight. By this time the security person was on her knees in front of me and using a magnetometer wand in the general area of the family jewels. John, standing behind her (so she couldn't see him) began making suggestive/obscene motions until I began to laugh. Not having a sense of humor or even understanding the reason for my laughter the security person became even more hostile. She ordered me to take off my shoes, belt, watch, and rings and even threatened a complete strip search right there in the terminal. I was finally able to make it through the metal detector and effect my escape, to the sounds of John laughing hysterically.

We finally made it to our gate and boarded the plane, a brand new seven-thirty-seven. As we sat and planned our next adventure we noticed some unusual activity around the cockpit. When a guy wearing a tool belt arrived we knew something serious was up. After much discussion and scratching of heads the tool man left. The Captain came on the intercom and announced that, although it was a brand new airplane there was a warning light that they couldn't get to go out. Rather than take a chance they were going to send the plane to the hangar for diagnostics and put us on another plane. We were given a gate number and told that that plane would be departing in twenty minutes. A mad dash ensued. We reached our new gate en-mass. The place was in chaos. Apparently, that plane was just about to board when they informed the passengers that they were all being bumped to accommodate us. A near riot ensued. There were several very vocal gentlemen who began to threaten violence. We couldn't stand by and watch this so John and I placed ourselves between the airline personnel and the mob. After trying to reason with them we finally resorted to threats of our own directed toward the most vocal of the group. We were able to get things settled down enough for boarding to commence. Once all of the passengers from our original flight were seated they began to fill the empty seats with passengers from the bumped flight. Sure enough the bigmouth was seated right between us. Being a big mouth he would not be satisfied with the accommodations he had and he continued to complain loudly. In fact, he became so obnoxious that the Flight Attendant asked him to leave the plane. Here we go again. John and I "assisted" him back to the terminal and the flight finally departed.

On this flight we had the same seating arrangement (thanks to our friend's sudden departure). This time I drew a face on the barf bag with the words "peanuts please" on it. We placed this on the center seat. When the Flight Attendant came around with the refreshments I mentioned that my friend Sam Barf was a big peanut eater. Not having the generous personality of our previous Flight Attendant she smiled and gave John and me our peanuts but none for Sam. A new strategy was needed. As we were seated in the exit row I spoke up and said, "John, I'm feeling pretty weak from lack of food, how about you?" John went along saying he couldn't remember the last time he ate. I then continued, *"You know, I'm not sure I have the strength to open that heavy emergency door if there was a problem."* Our Flight Attendant got the message; she reached beneath the refreshment cart and pulled out a large bag full of peanut packs. She handed me the whole bag, it must have contained thirty or forty bags of peanuts. *"Do you think this will be enough to get you through the flight?"* she asked with a grin. We ate peanuts for the rest of the trip and had some left over when we got home.

We finally arrived in Salt Lake City around nine p.m. and rented a car. We traveled on a two lane road up through the mountains when suddenly up ahead I saw a girl standing in the road with a Stop sign. As I began to slow down I wondered if this was how they ambushed you up here in militia country. It seemed very strange for a girl to be alone on top of a mountain late at night holding a Stop sign. Of course being law abiding citizens we stopped and asked what was going on. She told us that they were doing some blasting to widen the road ahead.

Sure enough a few minutes later we heard the explosion and felt the mountain shake. We sat there talking for about a half hour mostly hearing about the resentment harbored against the Mormons who travelled to Jackson Hole to party and raise Cain. Apparently they had a saying, "GOD can't see over the Tetons!"

We had a very eventful week visiting the great state of Wyoming. After nearly starting a bar brawl over a pool game, risking life and limb around the hot springs and geysers of Yellowstone and nearly running into a buffalo that was standing in the middle of the road (covered in snow) as we returned from

Cheyenne we successfully returned to Salt Lake City to catch our flight to San Francisco.

On the first Friday night in town we went on a ride along in the Tenderloin District. The Tenderloin District is akin to Baltimore's Block but much larger. It was Sodom & Gomorrah in miniature (I fear that since those days it has spread to all parts of the country).

Just to give you an idea of the "flavor" of the Tenderloin District I quote from the *SFGate* web site, *"Repeatedly described in most tourist guides as "the worst neighborhood in San Francisco," the Tenderloin thrives despite its bad rap. Sure, there are Tenderloin loads of drug dealers, addicts, prostitutes and mentally unstable street people, but if you can get past that, you'll find it is also one of the city's most exciting and diverse locales. Getting its funky, florid nickname from the days when policemen were paid more to work its mean streets, thereby affording the cops better cuts of meat, the Tenderloin is moving up these days."*

The police sub-station was in the basement of the bank once held up by Patty Hearst (you younger readers may have to Google her – pretty interesting story). The huge bank vault was still there with its door gaping open. We were told that several suspects decided to confess after being threatened with "the vault". You see, no one in the department had the combination so incarceration would be for life! An interesting aside – the building had been bought by a Chinese company. The City had been leasing it for $10,000 an month or something ridiculous. After the sale went through they never heard from the new owners so they had in effect become "squatters" – staying rent free.

We met with Sergeant Al Yee who showed us around the station, explained a bit about the Tenderloin District and then took us out to see for ourselves. Now, John and I were not naïve by any means, but this was an eye opener. One of the first things we noticed was the proliferation of homeless people wondering the streets. There was one particularly interesting looking fellow with a boom box strapped to his chest. John was fascinated by him so he jumped out, put his arm around the guy and told me to take a picture. The guy stopped John and demanded five dollars for the privilege! John complied with a laugh and I took the picture.

We had just finished with the homeless guy when we were flagged down by a frantic man in his mid-twenties. He was almost in tears as he explained that he had been in the "Peep Show" booth and run out of quarters.

He went to the front of the establishment to replenish his supply and had left his horn in the booth. When he returned it was gone!

He ran back to cover the front entrance and saw us passing by. He demanded that we go in and turn the place upside down and find his horn!

Reluctantly we entered the establishment and informed the manager of the situation. He was very cooperative and gave us a master key that opened the viewing rooms and told us to search to our heart's delight – with the stipulation that any illegal activity on the part of the patrons was not the responsibility of the establishment. So, Sgt. Yee set off followed by John, me and the victim. The things we saw in those booths were both funny and disgusting. Sergeant Yee would knock, announce his presence and then, if the door was not opened he would use the key. In many cases these booths were being used as cheap "quickie" room by gay men who had met in one of the many bars in the area. The reactions to being confronted by the police and an entourage ran the gamut from surprise to terror to invitations to join them.

After subjecting ourselves to this for a time John and I let Sgt. Yee finish on his own (we were close by if he needed backup). Unfortunately the poor fellow did not recover his beloved horn. A theft report was taken and we were on our way. We saw and heard many things on the mean streets of San Francisco that night, none of which I intend to relate here. If you are that curious you can go check it out for yourself.

While we're on the topic of spreading goodwill I'll relate a story of my exploits in Chicago around that same time.

In May of every year the Fraternal Order of Police hosts "Police Week" in Washington DC. It's a time to meet fellow officers from all over the country and it culminates in a ceremony honoring those who lost their lives in the line of duty  during the previous year. In May of 1996 I met Ron Santos a Detective from the Chicago Police Department. Ron's attending the memorial had special significance for him as he was almost one of the honorees. He had been shot at close range nine times while investigating a case the previous year. Now, it's not unusual for cops to be shot during investigations (unfortunately it happens all too often). What was unusual was that he was an Internal Affairs detective and the "suspect" that shot him was the cop he was investigating!

I'll regress a bit to tell his story as he told it to me. Ron had always wanted to be a cop. He worked hard, kept his nose clean and was accepted by the Chicago PD when he turned twenty-one. It did not take him long to become disillusioned. Apparently he had a very high regard for the PD and his expectations were not met by reality. As a result he decided to help clean up the corruption he had so sadly witnessed. He applied to the Internal Affairs Division and was accepted.

When he informed me that he was assigned to the Narcotics Section of IAD I was taken aback. We had no such thing in Baltimore! Interestingly, in his interview he was asked how he felt about cops stealing money from drug dealers.

His answer got him the job in Chicago and would have gotten him fired in Baltimore. He said if the officers had gone on a raid and confiscated a large quantity of drugs and money he had no problem with them using some of the money to buy pizza and beer while they completed their extensive paperwork! To each his own.

Ron shared another interesting story with me that I feel compelled to repeat here. Interstate I-90 runs through Chicago. The City was feeling the economic pinch and the resulting manpower shortage so they made an agreement with the Illinois State Police to patrol I-90 within the city limits. This arrangement had only been in place a few weeks when Ron got caught up in it. He was running late for work and was speeding down I-90 when a State Trooper pulled him over. Ron was in uniform then so when the Trooper approached Ron expected some degree of "professional courtesy". The Trooper had other ideas. The conversation went something like this:

"Sir, I stopped you for exceeding the posted speed limit - license and registration please."
"Yeah – sorry but I'm running late for my shift, I'll slow it down."
"I asked for your license and registration please."
"Okay, look I said I'd slow it down now just let me get on to my station so I can get to work."
"I don't care who you are or where you are going; I need your license and registration."
"Let me ask you something Trooper. If you need a backup in the City who comes?"

"Chicago PD – there aren't enough State guys in the area."
"Exactly – so now I'm going to get out of my car, punch you in the nose

and kick your butt all over this highway. When your backup gets here it will be my shift and they will probably help me stuff you into your trunk!"

The Trooper glared at him for a long moment and then said, *"Just slow it down okay?"* and Ron continued on to work.

At any rate Ron invited me to visit his department if I ever got up to Chicago and we exchanged business cards. A few months later I was assigned to attend a conference in Chicago so I made arrangements to meet him when I got there.

This particular conference was addressing new police radio systems; and as I was a key member of the planning team for Baltimore's new system it was important information to have. I was accompanied by Battalion Chief Mike Kernan who was my counterpart on the Fire Department. I enjoyed traveling with Mike but was not thrilled to learn that the City was cutting costs so we had to share a hotel room.

Once we arrived in Chicago we were met by a Motorola rep and taken to dinner. He chose a place called "Dick's Last Resort" on the Navy Pier. This was a very unusual establishment. The staff made it a point to be as rude as possible but make it funny at the  same time. I got some idea what we were in for when we walked in and stood waiting to be seated.

The "hostess" looked at us and said, "What are you morons doing, go sit down, do I have to do everything for you?" I sort of got right into it (cops are good at being rude) but Mike is such a truly nice guy he was out of his element. Our waitress lost no time in zeroing in on the easy prey. When she came back with our order she kept winking at Mike.

The French Fries were served in a small metal pail. I asked our waitress if their food was so bad that they provided barf buckets with it. We had a laugh about that when suddenly she sat down next to Mike and put her arm around him. *"You like me don't you"* she cooed. *"I know you like me; you keep smiling at me every time I walk by"*. Well, Mike was dumbfounded. He turned three shades of red and just sat there fumbling for words while we all had a good laugh. Once dinner was finished Mike headed off to the nearest fire house and I went to meet Ron. The conference was to start bright and early the next morning.

I met Ron and he proceeded to show me around some of the hot spots of Chicago. We hit a couple of bars and had a few drinks while trading "war stories". As we were heading out to another of his favorite spots we passed a night club with a line in front. I asked him what the place was like and he responded,

"I don't know, I've heard it's a pretty lively joint but I can't afford the cover charge of $35."
You're kidding me right? This is Chicago, you're a Chicago cop and you pay a cover charge to get into a night club? Find a place to park, get your badge ready and follow me."

We walked up to the bouncer in front of the place and I pulled out a mug shot and held it in front of him while Ron flashed his badge.

"You seen this guy here tonight?" I asked

Without even focusing on the photo he replied that he never saw the guy before in his life.

"I hope for your sake that's the truth. We're going in and look around for him, and if we find him you're going downtown with him, you understand?"

The bouncer took a long look at the photo and then answered,

"I don't know, I see hundreds of people every night. Go on in and look but if you find him it's not my problem, ok?"

With that we entered and were having a pretty good time until the bouncer found us and pointed to a guy on the dance floor and said, *"Isn't that your guy?"*

Needless to say we had to at least make it look as if we were interested. After careful consideration we told him it did not look as if we would find him there and left. From there we went to another drinking establishment that was a bit quieter. It is said that time flies when you are having fun – well when last call came I thought it was nearing two a.m. (when bars close in Baltimore). I looked at my watch and found that it was almost six a.m. (when bars close in Chicago)! I was just entering the hotel room when Mike's alarm went off and it was time to get ready for the conference. I think Mike got a bit more out of the information presented than I did.

I heard from Ron a few months later that he had shared my little mug shot trick with some of his closest colleagues and they were all using it!

ENEMIES IN HIGH PLACES

Just so you don't think that I was a complete moron stumbling my way through my career I thought I'd give an example of some decent police work. This story begins in early May 1985. I had recently received the American Legion Police Officer of the Year Award for Baltimore City. I had taken the lieutenant's exam and came out in the top ten. I was on top of my game. Little did I know then just where doing my job would land me.

My brother-in-law (Bevis) worked in the Mayor's Office of Manpower. He supervised many of the city's warehouses. One evening he called me at home and asked if I could drop by his house and discuss a matter that had him very concerned. When I arrived, he proceeded to explain to me that his boss (John Cullom) had been making some rather odd purchases lately. Bevis had overheard conversations over the past few weeks regarding the house that Mr. Cullom was building just outside the city. That morning he had overheard his boss giving directions over the phone for delivery of a furnace. He had also given a city purchase order number to the company. The directions were for a location outside the city. I asked Bevis if he could locate the purchase order for the furnace so we could investigate this further. He said that he would search for one the next day. Several times during our conversation he stressed that Mr. Cullom was on the Mayor's cabinet and as such, he was a very powerful (and well connected) man.

He was worried that if I went to my superiors that Mr. Cullom would hear about it and the investigation would be quashed. I promised to keep it to myself.

The next morning he called me and told me that he had found the purchase order and it confirmed his suspicions. The order was for a furnace that would burn wood, coal, gas or oil. It was from a company in New Jersey that was not on the city's approved vendors list. The order did not list the address but did show a delivery date and time just two days hence. As we knew the furnace was coming from New Jersey and going to the Timonium area it was easy to determine the route it would take. They had to go south on I-95 and then west on 695 (Beltway) to I-83. I could set up surveillance somewhere along Rt. 695 near I-83 and wait for the truck. The only hitch in my plan was if the delivery truck was unmarked. Just to be safe I called the company and represented myself as the contractor on-site. I told him I wanted to be sure not to miss the truck and asked if it would have the company name on it. He assured me that it would.

The morning of delivery (off duty, on my own time and out of my jurisdiction), I set up on a bridge overlooking the Beltway. To appear a little less obvious I raised my hood so as not to draw too much attention. They say you can never find a cop when you need one; conversely there is always one around when you don't. Naturally, as I'm standing next to my car watching the beltway for the truck a Baltimore County unit stops behind me to investigate the problem.

Just then I see the delivery truck approaching. I have no choice but to do something that all cops hate. I run toward his car before he can get out. I don't want to reach into my pocket for my badge as I'm running toward him as, even if my running at him didn't spook him, he would definitely perceive this as a threat. I quickly explain that I am a Baltimore City cop working in plain clothes. Only then do I pull out my badge. Once he sees this I run back to the car and take off after the truck. By this time I have lost sight of him. I speed and weave in and out of traffic trying to catch up to him. So far, nothing. I pass an exit and begin to worry. Suppose he got off there? I have no choice but to keep on. I pass another exit and begin to get really anxious. Still I press on. Just before the next exit I spot him ahead and fall in behind him. When I observed him turn in to a construction site, I continue on until I find a place to leave the car and walk back. From a vantage point in the bushes, I photograph the delivery. Now all we could do is wait. Until the furnace is actually paid for with city funds, no law had been broken. While I'm waiting I do a property search and verify that the house under construction does in fact belong to Mr. Cullom.

We expected the invoice to be paid in four to six weeks so I told Bevis to keep an eye on things and call me when it had been paid. It turned out that he could not be patient that long. One morning about three weeks after the delivery, I received a call from a State Police Sergeant in Timonium informing me that he had Bevis in his office. Apparently, Bevis was worried that the investigation would be compromised so he wanted to turn it over to the State Police. I explained to the Sergeant that the crime (if one was committed) was within the city's jurisdiction and that I had it covered. He agreed and sent Bevis on his way. Needless to say I was very agitated about Bevis getting me involved in this and then insinuating that I could not handle it properly. We had a long discussion on the matter and came to an understanding (or so I thought).

I had just gotten into bed and dropped off to sleep after a long and busy midnight shift. The phone rang around nine a.m. and woke me up. When I answered I was shocked to be talking to the City Comptroller. He said he would appreciate it if I would come to his office immediately. If I had a problem with  that he would call the Police Commissioner and have him order me to do so. I told him there was no need for that and that it would take me about an hour to get dressed and get down there. When I arrived, I was not surprised to find Bevis in the Comtroller's office. Once again my brother-in-law felt the need to jump the gun and involve someone else. What he expected to gain with this I had no idea. The Comtroller summarized the conversation he had had with Bevis and informed me that he would see to it that the Mayor handled the matter personally. He assured us that the Mayor would not stand for such behavior. Bevis seemed to be satisfied with this course of action, I was not. I had done some digging into Mr. Cullom's background while I was waiting for the invoice to be paid. I learned that Mr. Cullom had been in charge of the Armistead Gardens Housing Project prior to coming to work for the

Mayor. Although never convicted, Mr. Cullom had been charged with stealing over $300,000 of the state funding over a five year period. This incident had been swept under the rug and Mr. Cullom was allowed to move on without consequence. I informed the Comtroller that I did not trust the Mayor to handle this matter as he had to have known that Cullom was a thief when he hired him. Great career move right? Anyway, I insisted that, regardless of what the Comtroller did, I would seek a warrant for Mr. Cullom as soon as I left the meeting. This placed the Comptroller in a very awkward spot. He did the only thing he could do; he called the State's Attorney for Baltimore City and asked that he see me immediately. I took the documentation that Bevis had brought along and went to meet with the State's Attorney. He was ecstatic when I presented my case. He immediately summoned a couple of investigators attached to his office to assist me in continuing the investigation. Now that the cat was out of the bag there was no need to be subtle. We seized all of Mr. Cullom's files from his office, subpoenaed his bank and phone records and obtained search warrants for the house he had under construction.

The investigation lasted several weeks and ended with a fifty-eight count indictment for theft of $1.2 million. Not only had he ordered the furnace; he had also had the heat pumps in his condo in Ocean City replaced and filled a warehouse in east Baltimore with all kinds of goodies.

The Mayor was publicly embarrassed by the incident. It was brought out that he had indeed hired Mr. Cullom after the scandal at Armistead Gardens. The Police Commissioner was embarrassed because a major case had been broken without his knowledge. This did not ingratiate me with these powerful men. The Mayor went on to become Governor. The State's Attorney went on to become Mayor. The Police Commissioner went on to become the Director of Public Safety for the State of Maryland and the city Comtroller was elected as the State Comptroller. Even Bevis received the first Outstanding Service Award ever presented by the city. Me? I went nowhere. From that point on I was "not suitable for promotion". No matter how many times I took the promotional exam, or how high I scored, I was always passed over with no official reason given.

NOT QUITE THE END

Once I retired from the department in June 1999 I thought my law enforcement days were over. However, I was fortunate enough to find employment that allowed me to use my accumulated wisdom and experience. I was speaking at a Mobile Data User Group conference shortly before I retired and ran into Tim Boyle. I had worked with Tim in the Southeast District in the 1970's but lost track of him when he moved on to another job. He was now a Captain at the Maryland National Capital Park Police – Montgomery County. He just happened to be looking for someone with my technical expertise and offered me a job. As a result I became the Systems Administrator for Mobile Data at the MNCPP. That lasted a bit more than a year. When Tim retired and moved on he asked me to come to work for his new company. So, in 2001 I was hired as a Subject Matter Expert by *PSComm* a public safety/technology consulting firm. You may notice there are not very many humorous stories after I retired from the police department. It is a simple fact of life, with age and wisdom come boredom. Once I entered the private sector I was expected to project a professional demeanor at all times. Clients expect results not practical jokes for their money. I can, without hesitation state that my consulting career was enjoyable and interesting. I was greatly enriched by the projects I undertook and the people I had the pleasure to work with. I have included a brief account of several of those projects in an effort to wrap things up as it were.

WASHINGTON DC

I had a rather inauspicious start to my consulting career. My first project dealt with restructuring a pharmaceutical company (right up my alley right?). I rarely even took prescription drugs let alone understand how they are manufactured and distributed. I plodded along as best I could until something I knew how to deal with came up and I got assigned to it.

The Metropolitan Police in Washington DC had recently purchased and installed three hundred Mobile Data Computers (MDC). In a complete disconnect, the Technology section installed them but the Administrative section did not institute any guidelines for their use. On top of that no user manuals were supplied nor was training given. It all came to a head when the police chief walked up on an officer to ask how he liked his new computer and found him viewing porn!

I was very familiar with the software package installed on the MDCs so I began putting together a training course and guidelines for use. One afternoon while looking at the user logs on the server I noticed a disturbing trend. Not only was profanity rampant but I saw several messages that on face value appeared to point to illegal activity. I reported my findings to the IT Manager and he took them immediately to the police chief. The next evening the Chief held a press conference with the Mayor and promised that a thorough investigation would ensue and heads would roll. That was easy for them to say, I had pulled over eight million transactions off the server! It would be my job to sift through them, determine which appeared to violate policy (which didn't exist) or were criminal. I was then to document them and turn them over to the Office of Professional Responsibility (Internal Affairs) for investigation. I was given a desk in the Technology section of OPR and went to work. Needless to say, with that many records I would become very familiar with Microsoft Access. I was fortunate enough to share an office with Detective Dewey Watkins who was an expert and taught me many trick and shortcuts to make my life easier.

The investigation went on for two years and towards the end I was tasked with monitoring current activity as well to make sure the new policy was being adhered to. It quickly became evident that the cops were messing with me.

We had created a search macro to find certain key words automatically (there was a total of one hundred fifty-two of them). Officers began sending messages that would cause an alert but upon investigation would be harmless. Here is an example:

"We'll teach them - We'll kill them in their house!"

The rest of the story – the Washington Redskins were going to Dallas for a football game that week.

Some (who must have had inside information) get even more creative. In another case I had discovered a message that indicated some black officers may have been targeting white males in a certain area. While that was being investigated I found this in the log:

I have a friend named whitey. He likes to hunt. We call him "huntin' Whitey".

That officer was politely asked to knock off the unnecessary chatter.

When all was said and done, after untold OPR man-hours and $185,000 for my services they charged one person. That's right one poor Lieutenant was reprimanded for – are you ready – allowing someone else to use his password!

I left them with manuals, guidelines and training and trained a new systems administrator to monitor things and went on to my next project.

DOTHAN & DETROIT

As the Washington DC project was ending I had the good fortune to be assigned to a cutting edge interoperability project involving the U.S. Secret Service; U.S. Park Police; U.S. Capital Police and the DC Metropolitan Police. I won't bore you with the details (especially since cutting edge then sounds like everyday stuff now). Overall it was interesting but boring. The best part was that the customers decided that the best place for a live test was the Super Bowl. Who am I to argue?

I had two projects going at once for a while. One was a racial profiling study for the city of Dothan Alabama (peanut capital of the world). There had been accusations that the Dothan PD was stopping and questioning blacks at a disproportionate rate to whites. It was the purpose of the study to determine if this was  the case and to institute steps to ensure it did not take place moving forward.

It did not take long to prove that the stops were justified and backed up by reasonable suspicion in the great majority of cases. We used what was then cutting edge technology (and costly in both officer time and city money) to alleviate a problem that never existed.

The second project was to assist the city of Detroit write their Homeland Security Plan. After 9/11 everyone was

scrambling to create a plan to deal with terrorism. The city of Detroit had no clue how to begin. Their first effort consisted on listing all gasoline and propane stations as possible targets. The Fermi - 2 Nuclear Power Plant and the Windsor Tunnel connecting the US and Canada escaped their notice. The first meeting that was set up to be inclusive of all concerned really set the stage for the whole project.

The conference center of a Detroit Hilton Hotel was booked for one hundred fifty attendees. The city was providing breakfast and lunch as well as a secure Wi-Fi network and laptops at each table to facilitate dissemination of information and communications. I received notice of the time and place and was asked to participate. I arrived two hours early (as I had to fly in from Maryland) and watched as the preparations were completed. They were serving breakfast starting at eight a.m. and the conference was to start at nine a.m. By eight-thirty I was starting to worry. After the tech guys left I was the only one there. At a little after nine a.m. I called the organizer to ask where everyone was. His response was, "Oh was that today? Let me check and get back to you." He called back ten minutes later and informed me that he had forgotten to e-mail the invitations so he would reschedule it for another time!

The final Homeland Security Plan was completed and presented to the city a couple of months later (with very little input from them). I am happy to say they have not, as of this writing had to use it (if they could even find it again).

MERRY OLD ENGLAND

My final project with *PSComm* was also my most interesting. It involved my going to London England to work with the New Scotland Yard on issues of crime prevention and traffic control.

It all came up rather suddenly so I had a rush to get a passport and arrange the trip. Phase One of the project was to demonstrate the technology we had supplied to the US Secret Service. At the same time we were to discuss the terrible crime wave they were having on the Underground (their subway). It seems that the wayward youth of London had stooped to  graffiti! They were "tagging" the trains when they stopped at certain stations. It then became a competition; once a train was tagged it was a target for every delinquent with a spray can. We came up with a two pronged attack that everyone agreed would work. It was put into operation a month later and within three months the problem was solved. I think the hardest part of this one was the language barrier. There is a saying that we are two people separated by a common language. I experienced that first hand (anyone out there know what a "skip" is in London – we call them dumpsters).

Lest we think that all of the Brits are very prim and proper I shall relate a brief "war story" from our brothers across the pond that fits nicely into this literary work. Although overall that rigid stereotype remained intact the exceptions were the actual street cops (Bobbies) I had the pleasure to meet. From my experience cops are cops the world over. All that I have met have shared the same morbid sense of humor and propensity to indulge in a bit of fun at the expense of their colleagues. The next story sounds like something I might have done if I had thought of it.

Constable Clive Davies was not well liked. He was constantly putting on airs (even for a Brit) and talking down to his colleagues. One day Clive came to work in a brand new red MG Midget. He had been dreaming about and saving for this car for years. He also had been bragging to his mates about it incessantly. As it was unusual for a lowly "copper" to be able to afford a new car in those days it made it all the more difficult to swallow. Finally, after a few days of having their noses rubbed in it the lads hatched a plan.

They waited until the weekend when everything was nice and peaceful. Constable Davies was on bicycle patrol and safely away from the station. One of the lads asked for a stolen check on a red MG he was following on Thorpe Hwy. The dispatcher came back with "no stolen" and listed to a Clive Davies. He then radioed in that he was trying to stop the vehicle but it was now traveling at a

high rate of speed to avoid him. Constable Davies jumped on the radio and excitedly informed everyone that it was his vehicle and to be very careful not to damage it. The fake chase went on for some time with Constable Davies trying to join in on his bicycle. Each time they would get close to his location the "chase" took a turn in another direction. They could tell by his winded radio messages that Clive was about worn out. It was then that they radioed in that the vehicle had gone off the road and into St. Anne's Lake. Clive, audibly upset said he was responding, asking if someone could pick him up on their way there. To the horror of all involved the Chief Superintendent (who was supposed to be safely at home with the family) came on the radio and said he was responding and would pick Clive up!

Of course the Chief Superintendent and Clive arrive at the lake and find no one there. Puzzled they ask for a better location. The lads simply ask the CS to meet them at the station and all will be made clear. After several hours of explanations and writing reports the lads  were sent back out to work. That no one was fired over this was a tribute to the CS as well as his understanding of just how grading Clive could be.

Some of us remember doing things for expediency sake. Why fill out all of those reports and waste all that time when nothing would ever come of it?

This next story brings back some of those memories. Those of you who lived it, put yourself in the place of these British cops. Remember, no sidearm, no shotgun, just you, a short stick and a lot of nerve.

The English Bobbie as you probably know was armed with only a truncheon (14" night stick). This was fine as an offensive weapon but was really lacking 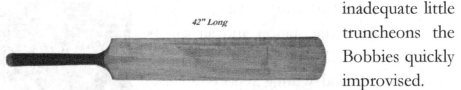 when it came to defense. Sergeant Phil (last name omitted to protect the guilty) had been on the force for thirty years when I met him. He told me of a time when he and some of his chaps had a bit of a row with some of the local riffraff in the south of London in the 1970's. He had come upon a large street fight and called for assistance. The situation quickly turned nasty when the gang decided it would be more fun to fight the Bobbies than each other. The Bobbies were outnumbered but what made matters worse was that the hooligans were armed with cricket bats. Having only their inadequate little truncheons the Bobbies quickly improvised.

42" Long

The window of a furniture store had already been broken out so several of the Bobbies broke the legs off of some tables and used them to good advantage! This near riot went on for some time until the ruffians retreated, carrying off their injured colleagues. Sgt Phil and his boys, having suffered no serious injuries dispersed and went about their business as if nothing had happened. No arrests, no reports, nothing!

Now be honest, those of you who served "back in the day", does any of this seem familiar?

The next phase of the project demanded a three month stay on site. They provided a rented house for me in the Earl's Court section of London. It was a very interesting house. The first floor contained a living room, dining room and small kitchen. Each of the two upper floors contained a bedroom and a bathroom. The entire house was "carpeted" with what appeared to be wicker. There was a very nice "garden" behind the house (to the British any green space behind the house is a garden. We simply call them back yards). I commented to someone that I was surprised by the size of the open spaces back there. It was almost like a small park. I was told that there had been a block of houses back there until World War Two when a German bomb took them out.

I had always heard that the one thing you could depend on in London was rain. The city is often depicted in movies and books as wet and dreary. I just happened to visit during the worst heat wave in recorded history. During my entire stay it only rained once (I got tired of carrying an umbrella by that time so of course I got drenched). Several weather records were broken while I was there, including the UK's highest recorded temperature 101.3 °F on August tenth. According to the BBC around two thousand more people than usual died in the United Kingdom during the 2003 heat wave. To help you better understand how unusual this was you have to realize that the vast majority of buildings in London are not air conditioned.

I was only able to find a couple of restaurants with air conditioning and these I frequented on the hottest evenings. If you want to have some fun ask for iced tea at a restaurant in England – they act as if you've insulted the Queen.

The biggest inconvenience I was forced to deal with was getting back and forth to the office on the Underground. The subway cars are not air conditioned and are always packed shoulder to shoulder during rush hour. To make things worse they decided that the tracks were too hot and may buckle if the trains went at normal speed so they slowed them to a crawl. My usual fifteen minute commute turned into forty-five minutes of sweltering misery.

The Greater London Urban Area is the second-largest in the European Union with a population of 9.8 million. There were six thousand traffic lights in London and the CCTV system had twenty-one thousand cameras installed. The newly formed LTCC was a merger of the Transport for London and the New Scotland Yard cameras. All of these camera feeds were to be available for display on a large video wall. With the aid of some new software the traffic light timing could be modified to expedite traffic flow. This was all coordinated with the buses and traffic wardens. When traffic in a specific area began to back up it would be called in to the 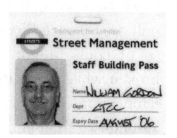 LTCC and using the traffic cameras as a guide the traffic lights would be adjusted to clear things up. I was also provided with an office in the newly formed Transport for London building.

Suddenly, I was the Deputy Director of the London Traffic Control Center!

In order to better understand how traffic was coordinated I stopped a Traffic Warden while I was out at lunch on my first day. I had a very informative conversation with him. He was pointing out the "No Parking" zones and how they were designated. I asked him what they did if someone parked in them illegally. He looked at me as if I had just escaped the Looney bin. The idea that a British citizen would disobey the Queen's parking regulations seemed completely foreign to him.

During an afternoon meeting with the Director and several of the New Scotland Yard brass I commented on my conversation with the Traffic Warden. I got that look again, "What do you mean you spoke with a Traffic Warden? We don't speak to Traffic Wardens!" was the reply. I wasn't sure if they felt it was beneath them to talk to a lowly Traffic Warden or if they were intimated by them. "Well, it's a good thing I didn't know any better because I got a lot of useful information from him. I can see several areas where the initial assumptions for the project are misguided" I replied.

We then went on to modify our approach and I believe made significant improvements to the system based on just one conversation with someone who was actually out there doing the job.

After business hours and on weekends I made a concerted effort to see as much of merry old England as I could. I took in all of the typical tourist attractions in London and then branched out to bus tours to various castles and historic sites.

During one of those memorable excursions I went to Warwick Castle. Attacked in 1264, besieged in 1642 and damage by fire in 1871, the Castle has nevertheless survived the ever-

changing fortunes of history. The first castle to appear on the site was a wooden mote and bailey constructed in 1068 at the command of William the Conqueror. It was my good fortune to attend during a joust. With all of the pomp and circumstance the British can muster an exciting show was in store for all! As the knights began to enter the courtyard area a jester (female) riding a donkey rode to the center and began to inform everyone what was about to take place.

She was very funny and got everyone in a festive mood. The knights in their brightly colored costumes began to prance their mighty steeds in front of the crowd. The jester then announced that it was customary for the ladies to present a token to the knight of her choice who would then go into battle  for her. She said a token could be anything from a scarf or hankie to an item of lingerie. Everyone laughed at this and most thought nothing of it. Most that is except one cute six year old girl. As the black knight stopped in front of her and held out his lance she hung her little cotton panties on the end. This was  followed by a roar of laughter and then a ghastly scream as her mother realized what she had done! I could hear the little girl protest, *"But mummy, she said lingerie. That means panties, right?"*

I thoroughly enjoyed this project and felt I had made a real difference by the time I headed home. Shortly after this project however *PSComm* dissolved and the partners went on to bigger and better things. I decided I had had enough of jetting around the world so I sold my house in Maryland and moved to Tennessee to retire once and for all.

ATLANTA

I had been "retired" for about a year when I received an e-mail from the former business manager at *PSComm* (Dave McDonald) asking if I was interested in working on a project in Atlanta Georgia as an independent contractor. The city found itself in dire need of a new 9-1-1 center. I found this ironic as I had visited their center back in 1995 when Baltimore was in the planning stages on our new center. We looked to Atlanta as the cutting edge experts then and now they were looking to the Baltimore team at DiDonato Consulting (with me as a Subject Matter Expert) for expertise to build their new center. I agreed to a one year contract with an option for a second if necessary. The project was extensive and I did not see how we would complete it in one year.

The "dire need" turned out to be political in nature. It seems that a developer offered the City twenty million dollars for one of their old rundown buildings. They were going to convert it to high end condos and shops that would bring additional tax revenue to the City. The Mayor jumped at it. After the deal was signed she happened to ask what the building housed. Oh, only the 9-1-1 Center and Police/Fire Communications, no big deal. The order went out from the Mayor's Office – move the 9-1-1 Center. What? Move it? How do you do that Madam Mayor? Do you shut down 9-1-1 and Police Dispatch for a week or so while you move everything? Once again a politician acted before thinking.

The City now had to find a new location to house the 9-1-1 Center and Police/Fire Communications. As all of the equipment was nearly fifteen years old it all had to be replaced. This necessitated constructing not only a new center but an entire new Public Safety radio network! We had to locate a site, oversee design and construction of the 9-1-1 Center and at the same time design and install a new radio system. The project ended up taking over three years and costing ninety-two million dollars! The Mayor made a great deal for the citizens of Atlanta.

The project had a rocky start. The City had a very sensible regulation that a project could not receive approval unless the funds were set aside to cover it. The City Finance Department dutifully set aside money for the projected costs. A short time later, as the project had not started yet the money was taken out and assigned to another project. Once our project started there was no money in the account! I went nearly a year without being paid! We finally resolved that issue when another arouse. The Department of Information and Technology (DoIT) was in a shambles. We could get little cooperation from them and this was becoming a major issue.

One guy stepped up and shouldered the load, Darryl. He worked tirelessly and was making good progress when he received his layoff notice. That's right; the only guy working with us was to be sent packing by this forward

thinking bureaucracy. The one guy in City government that understood the issue was Bob Shelor. The Project Manager (Dan Engler) and Bob made arrangements to pay Darryl as a contractor and kept the work going while they pleaded with the City to hire Darryl back. They finally saw the light, however there was a problem (there always seems to be a problem). The rules for hiring had changed and Darryl no longer met the standards to be a City IT employee! Really? Thankfully this was resolved and Darryl was returned as the IT lead in the project.

Overall the Atlanta project was enjoyable and rewarding. I worked with a great bunch of folks and I am richer for the experience. I need not go into further detail about the shortcomings of politicians and the extreme inefficiency inherent in government.

BACK TO BALTIMORE

I was in Atlanta for the final post-operative meeting when I got a call from Allen Carr who had been a company rep for Aether when I worked for the Maryland National Capitol Park Police. He asked if I would have lunch with him while I was in Atlanta (how he knew I was there I'm not sure). It was arranged and he stopped by my hotel and picked me up. After he questioned me at length on the Atlanta project I began to feel that there was a purpose other than curiosity behind his questions. Sure enough he finally got to the point. Apparently he was searching for a Project Manager for a contract that his company had just signed with the Baltimore Police Department! It consisted of purchasing twenty-four hundred Blackberry

Smart Phones and installing Computer Aided Dispatch (CAD); National Crime Information Center (NCIC); Motor Vehicle Administration (MVA); Maryland State Criminal Justice Information System (CJIS) and Workforce Management software on them as well as setting up the servers.

So, here I was, full circle from BPD around the country and to Europe and now back where I started. The project called for three months on-site. I booked an Extended Stay hotel just a few blocks from the house I had lived in when I retired from BPD. I almost felt at home there (except for missing my dear wife terribly).

I arrived bright and early for the Kickoff meeting at BPD HQ. I was going over my material in the Management Information Systems (MIS) conference room when I heard a familiar voice. I looked up as three gentlemen entered the room, but I did not recognize any of them. As the meeting progressed I heard the familiar voice come from a member of the IT staff referred to as BJ. After the meeting I asked what BJ's last name was. It turned out that he was the son of one of the IT guys I use to work with years before. Same voice, same mannerisms, different face. It also turned out that the father (Bernie Lowry) had retired and returned as a contract worker at MIS. I had the pleasure of working with the father and son team for the project.

The MIS Director was (in my opinion) without exception the least IT qualified of any director I have met in all of my travels. No one I spoke with anywhere in the department could figure out how she got the job.

The one thing she was good at (as seems common among incompetents) was arrogance. This made my job more difficult  but also provided comic relief at times. Like the time she was addressing the Commissioner and Command staff. The Blackberry Smartphone is a product of Research in Motion (RIM). The Director stood up and in her explanation of the proposed product said they were buying, "Rhythm in Motion" phones. She said this as she made a gyrating motion (as if she was using a hula hoop). Some stifled laughter, others looked very puzzled.

I was provided with an office in the old MIS (the administrative section had moved out of the fourth floor and with the exception of the office I was given the area was used as a computer junkyard). Was there a message there?

This was to be another "cutting edge" project merging disparate technologies into a complete package to assist the officer in the field and provide data to Command for resource management.

The Department decided on "Side Partner" as the project name. The name stemmed from the fact that Baltimore has always used one-man patrols. Officers did not have a partner riding with them, their backup was the officer working the post next to them – hence "side partners". The Blackberry device connected to multiple databases to access live information on crime and suspects including warrants, driving records, stolen property and photographs.

The Department developed an in-house application it calls Priority Warrants. When officers log on to their device at the start of a shift, they are automatically given a list of the top ten warrants in the specific area they are covering on that particular day. The Side Partner also allows officers to take images from any crime scene they encounter during their shift. With the new device, officers can take images and download them when they return to the station.

In addition to accessing CAD, NCIC, CJIS, MVA and warrants the devices included software that tracked the officer from start to finish on their shift. This was the feature loved by the command staff and hated by the street cop.

Since the ability to track police cars first surfaced in the early 1990's it has been a point of contention. The early Automatic Vehicle Locators (AVL) used a small round ("hockey puck") antenna mounted on the deck inside the rear window. Officers would line a baseball cap with aluminum foil and place it over the antenna so they couldn't be tracked. When the antenna was moved to the trunk of the car, wires would mysteriously break on a routine basis. These devices even became issues in contract negotiations. One jurisdiction allowed the dispatcher to view the officer's location but forbade their supervisor from requesting the information! So, needless to say the rank and file was less than thrilled with their every move being watched. I was against them when I was a cop on the street; however my position "evolved" as I saw their potential. The number one benefit was officer safety.

I cannot count the number of times an officer was in serious trouble and was only able to call for help on the radio but not give his location. With this new technology help would arrive much more quickly and lives would be saved. A secondary benefit was resource allocation. When units can be assigned according to where they actually are rather than where they are supposed to be things run much more smoothly. One constant issue fought by supervisors was officers grouping up. If two or three officers are having coffee together then obviously the area they are assigned to is left unprotected. Precise locations, time of day and shift status of each officer with a Side Partner device are provided to dispatchers through Google Maps and the GPS mapping application. This feature came into play twice in the early stages of the project. In one an officer was accused of sexually assaulting a female during a traffic stop. She stated the assault lasted twenty minutes. The Side Partner logs show he was only at the location for five minutes (long enough to write the ticket she was trying to get out of). In the second case an officer was accused of excessive speed contributing to an accident. Once again the logs came to the rescue. They showed that he was in fact doing the speed limit when the crash occurred.

Another useful officer safety feature was "Hit Notification". When officers use the device to search for warrants and get 'a hit' the dispatcher will get the same information and every officer in his unit will also get notification that a live "hit" has been generated. This is extremely useful if an officer needs assistance in dealing with the suspect and is unable to call for help.

So, after three months of frustration (mostly caused by the State and arcane rules for connecting to their databases) the system was up and running. Everyone was happy and I was accused of doing an excellent job. So much so that InterAct asked me to be the Senior Project Manager for the State of Maryland CAD Interoperability project. I agreed but quickly discovered that I was not a good fit (we did not see eye to eye on some ethical issues). I agreed to assist until they found the right person for the job. I spent a few months getting the ball rolling until they hired a guy to take over. The last I heard the project was moving along slowly.

So there you have it. I went from innocent, wet behind the ears rookie to Senior Project Manager running the show in a mere thirty-six years. Who knows what the next thirty-six will hold.

THE MANY FACES OF RETIREMENT

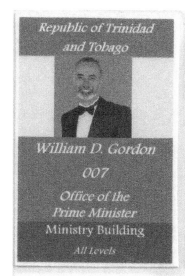

Republic of Trinidad
and Tobago

William D. Gordon

007

Office of the
Prime Minister

Ministry Building

All Levels

Contractor

WILLIAM D
GORDON
METROPOLITAN POLICE

NAME

CONTRACTOR
POSITION/TITLE

CHIEF OF POLICE

District of Columbia

PRESIDENTIAL RETREAT

CAMP DAVID

POLICE DEPARTMENT
CITY OF BALTIMORE. MARYLAND

William D Gordon

WHOSE SIGNATURE AND IDENTIFICATION
APPEARS HEREON HOLDS THE TITLE OF

Contractor MIS

Contract Employee

Expires   08/23/2010

CITY OF ATLANTA
RESURGENS
9-1-1
1965
ATLANTA, GA.
POLICE

ATLANTA POLICE

CONSULTANT

4473

BILL GORDON

CPSIA information can be obtained at www.ICGtesting.com
Printed in the USA
LVOW03s1152231114

415190LV00010B/315/P